Dr. Jeffrey L. Carson
&
Dr. Neenah Estrella-Luna

PROMISES MADE

The Resettlement of our Allies

Shirley St Publishing

Printed in the United States of America

Name: Jeffrey Carson & Neenah Estrella Luna
Title: Promises Made: The Resettlement of our Allies.
Description: First Edition | Shirley St Publishing |
Subjects: Immigration | U.S. Military | Laws and Policy
Identifiers: ISBN: 978-0-9988007-3-8

Shirley St Publishing
Independent Publishing
Wyoming, USA

This book and photos were reviewed and cleared by the Department of Defense on June 4th, 2018. The views expressed are those of the authors and do not reflect the official policy or position of the Department of Defense or the U.S. Government.

On June 1st, 2018, the contents of this book were reviewed and cleared by the U.S Department of State, Public Affairs. The following research does not represent the Department of State or its policies, or those of the U.S. Government.

Further, this research does not disclose or in any way allow the public to access classified information even if it is already publicly available due to a previous unauthorized disclosure.

Table of Contents

Acknowledgements

From Jeff Carson

To the foreign nationals, men and women, who have sacrificed alongside America's men and women: Thank you! We have not always reciprocated your sacrifice with a helping hand but I hope this small project can further the cause and improve future resettlements.

To the men and women of the U.S. government who are on the front lines of processing and resettling foreign nationals: Your advocacy, tireless – and sometimes thankless – work, and sacrifice has led to generations of Americans. Through the years, the newly arrived Americans will serve in industries across our country and their contribution to society is a small piece of gratitude to your work.

To retired Major Mike Bell: You served your country in a time of war. Your wounds, aches, and pains will remind you of that in the years to come. I know of no other person who has served our country with more honor and courage than you. I look forward to telling my children what an honorable soldier and person you are. How you taught me so much and served with such distinguished pride. On behalf of a grateful nation-Thank you.

To Dr. Estrella-Luna. Without you, this work would have never made it outside the hallways of academia. Well done!

And finally, to my family: This book is a testament that a goal and dream can come true-Notwithstanding the support of a loving wife.

From Neenah Estrella-Luna

I must first thank my co-author, Dr. Jeffrey Carson, for asking me to join him on this journey. I was in the middle of an unplanned and unwelcome career adjustment when the offer of co-authorship came through. It was just what I needed for my own healing. I rediscovered the writer in myself through this process. Thank you.

The amazing immigration attorney, Matt Cameron, provided invaluable guidance on the history of the refugee system. The introduction would not be what it is without him. I am luck to count you as a neighbor and friend. Susan Church also provided guidance on current case law as it might apply to future refugees. Thank you both.

I must also thank my husband, Dr. Marcos Luna, for his unwavering support for all of the crazy adventures that I get myself into. He reads everything I write, even when he doesn't have time. I am very lucky to have you in my life. Thank you.

Finally, I must also thank my students at Salem State University for reminding me why books like this are important.

Prologue

2009

In 2009, Captain Jeffrey Carson deploys with other members of the Ohio Army National Guard to Afghanistan as an intelligence officer. He is part of an embedded training team consisting of US soldiers and Hungarian Defense Forces (HDF). They arrive in Baghlan province in the middle of June to relieve the previous team. On the three-hour drive to Camp Khilagay, Carson is distracted by the breathtaking scenery. He is surrounded by rugged mountains and scrubby vegetation. It looks nothing like Ohio, where he grew up, or the New England landscape he is now familiar with.

But he is not here for vacation. His mission during this deployment is to train Afghan National Army (ANA) soldiers in the reconnaissance platoon. The first week is busy with briefings and trying to suck up as much information as he can from his counterparts before they leave. He is told to have very low expectations about air or combat support, especially when they are out in the field. He also learns that the Afghan kandak (the equivalent of a battalion) that he will be working with has only received a couple of months of training. Among the many things emphasized to Carson, the most important is this: Shayan, his translator, is his greatest asset. Carson finds it hard to believe someone this young could be so critical to the work.

As soon as the previous team leaves, the platoon is ordered to do a patrol near a particular village in the area. This patrol will take them from their already remote outpost and expose them to who knows what. The team is still getting to know each other. No one knows the area or has contacts in this village, not even the ANA soldiers. But they have no choice. They have their orders. Out into the field for this first operation they go.

The unit successfully completes the patrol in three days. Everyone is exhausted but Carson is mindful that their mission is to train these ANA soldiers. The end of the operation provides a teachable moment to learn how to properly thank the village elders through humanitarian assistance. Providing an assistance package of food and gifts will send a positive message as they depart. Through this, they hopefully will gain the support of the elders and other members of the village. It is important for the ANA soldiers to understand that making friends with the village elders keeps them safe and allows them to gather intelligence. Doing this also extends the operation by a day, but Carson believes it is worth it.

After receiving approval for an assistance package, he puts the ANA soldiers in charge of informing the elders and media, contacting local leaders, and delivering the rice, blankets, soccer balls, and other nonperishable items to the village. The US will provide the materials but the Afghans must be the face of it.

Exhaustion sets in early the next morning. The days on patrol have been long and the nights have not provided for much rest. Everyone sleeps in alternating shifts either inside or on top of their vehicles. The idea of ending the operation with a humanitarian project sounded better the day before. When they all wake up on that last morning, no one wants to be out in the field a second longer than they need to.

Despite the fatigue, all goes well. Over 100 villagers, mainly women and children, show up to the village center. As the food and toys are being distributed, the mood lightens. The village elders are gracious. The children are ecstatic at receiving such simple gifts. The ANA soldiers do a spectacular job of looking professional and appear to take pride in being of service. Carson is proud.

Until he spots an ANA soldier and an Afghan National Police officer stealing some of the rice and soccer balls from the back of the container. Carson is now enraged. And sleep deprived. Anger and fatigue get the better of him and he screams at the two would-be thieves for 10 minutes until they put back everything they took. He walks away fuming, wanting nothing more than to wrap it all up, get back to Camp Khilagay, and get some sleep.

Fifteen minutes later, Shayan slides next to Carson and whispers in his right ear, "Sir, the Afghan you were yelling at is behind you. He's been there for about 10 minutes and he is about to shoot you." Carson looks over his shoulder and sees an Afghan soldier, Pasoon, pointing an AK-47 at him.

From the US perspective, Carson would be within his rights to shoot Pasoon in self-defense. But shooting him is actually the worst of few options. Pasoon has nothing to lose by shooting Carson. The US military are hardly the most popular people in Afghanistan. Pasoon would likely be praised for killing an American. Carson, on the other hand, would be subject to military investigations. Shooting Pasoon, no matter how well justified, would compromise his ability to train these ANA soldiers. It would also feed the suspicion that these foreigners (i.e., the US government and coalition forces) do not respect Afghans or Afghan culture.

So Carson tries diplomacy. Translating through Shayan, he explains that stealing is wrong and not how militaries behave. This only makes Pasoon angrier. Carson tries appealing to his self-interest and tells him that he will give him soccer balls and rice once they return to Camp Khilagay but that taking gifts in front of the villagers is not how soldiers behave. Pasoon is not backing down. Nothing Carson says can mollify the bruised ego of this ANA soldier.

Carson's break comes when other ANA soldiers see what is happening and come over. They first try to reason with Pasoon but he is not having it. Eventually, they wrestle the rifle away from him. Within minutes it is all over. None of the US or Hungarian soldiers see anything other than a scuffle amongst the Afghan soldiers.

Ten minutes later, the operation is over. They pack up and head back to Camp Khilagay. The return to camp is uneventful. Carson is annoyed, mainly with himself. He knows better than to publicly call out even justifiable transgressions. He has just gotten here. This was the first operation together and he had nearly got shot by an Afghan soldier that he would be living, training, and fighting with for the next several months. This was a big mistake. He feels stupid. He doesn't tell his leadership about it. He hopes it will just go away.

But it doesn't go away. Two days after returning to camp, Carson learns that Pasoon is threatening to kill Shayan. To Pasoon and others, Shayan is a traitor for warning Carson, a foreigner. It doesn't help that Shayan is Tajik, a minority group in Afghanistan, while Pasoon is Pashtun, the majority ethnic group.

Carson now truly understands how fragile the security situation truly is. He writes a note to his wife with his last words and carries it in his pocket for the remainder of this mobilization, something he had never done in any previous deployment. But he is more worried about his translator. Shayan has to leave the security of Camp Khilagay at the end of every workday.

Carson immediately informs the US and Hungarian commanders that Pasoon is threatening Shayan. In doing so, he also has to disclose the incident that started all of this, despite his embarrassment.

The ANA kandak commander simply dismisses the incident and

the threats to Shayan. He insists that Pasoon is a hard worker and waves away the threats as simply poor judgment. Carson presses his leadership to have Pasoon removed or at least disciplined. For a month, at Carson's insistence, the US leadership periodically meets with the kandak commander about Pasoon and each time come away with nothing. At one point, Carson forces his way into one of these meetings where he learns how deeply corrupt this commander actually is. In the kandak commander's room, Carson sees evidence of the practice of *bacha bazi*, the sexual enslavement of young boys common among warlords in the area. Pasoon, he learns, is part of the commander's inner circle and participates in the abuse of these young boys. Carson is horrified.

During the month that Carson is complaining about the kandak commander and Pasoon, he still has to work with his unit to prepare for the upcoming national elections. They are responsible for securing polling sites to ensure the credibility of the election. While he is working to protect Shayan, they are both still trying to do their jobs, Carson as an intelligence officer training a reconnaissance platoon and Shayan as his translator.

After about a month, it seems to Carson that no one at Camp Khilagay is able or willing to do anything about Pasoon or the kandak commander. It feels like he is fighting his own bureaucracy as much as the enemy. So he complains to the leadership at the headquarters in

Mazar-i-Sharif. Finally, someone takes it seriously. An internal investigation into the kandak commander uncovers even more corruption and incompetence than anyone was aware of. This is a major concern to the leadership because this unit is responsible for securing the polling sites in their area. Pasoon is discharged from the ANA. In addition, the kandak commander is removed with the kind of speed Carson never dreamed possible. He is replaced with an ethnic Tajik who takes his responsibility to build this kandak very seriously.

Both Carson and Shayan are relieved.

Freed from the direct threat of Pasoon and with a more effective kandak commander in charge, the remainder of Carson's deployment goes well. Shayan is by Carson's side through several combat, intelligence, and humanitarian projects. Intelligence operations move forward, which is Carson's mission. But it is providing humanitarian assistance that Carson remembers the best. The ANA delivers incubators to health facilities, yoga mats for a women's center, 300 classroom chairs to an agricultural university, and books to local elementary schools. Working together with the ANA platoon, they conduct reconnaissance and secure villages during the harvest. They dig wells in extremely remote villages as well as build relationships and networks to support an effective intelligence unit. It is the most gratifying work in Carson's 20+ year military career.

Through all of this, Carson gets to know his translator better.

Shayan, despite being a member of a minority group, belongs to a more educated and cultured class. Like many of the translators in Afghanistan, Shayan has above average levels of education and experience. Before working for the US coalition forces, he worked for an NGO providing medical supplies to hospitals. Shayan talks a lot about his mother but is reticent to talk about his sister. His greatest hope is for his country to simply function.

Shayan is also fearless, almost to a fault. This becomes evident when the platoon is ambushed on their way out to an operation. The platoon is heading down a narrow road in an area known to be problematic. Leading the platoon are the ANA soldiers in four Toyota pickup trucks, several sitting in the open bed of each of the trucks. Behind them are the US and HDF soldiers in four armored military vehicles. On the left is a ditch and ten foot walls with homes behind them. On the right are watermelon fields. The enemy is hiding in the fields. They could be Taliban, local insurgents, warlords, or drug traffickers. No one knows. As soon as the ANA trucks roll past a certain point, they are under fire. The ANA soldiers jump out of their trucks and dive into the ditch. Captain Mike Bell is leading this convoy and he orders the US and HDF soldiers to get out and return fire. The HDF soldiers refuse to leave the vehicle. In hindsight, Carson is not surprised by this. The Hungarians are in Afghanistan only to comply with their NATO obligations, not because they believe in the mission. They never hide their annoyance at having to be there. The HDF soldiers are competent but unwilling to put their lives on the line for the Afghans, who they hold in very low regard.

Bell orders Shayan to tell the ANA soldiers to get back in their vehicles, turn around, and return to camp. The US soldiers will provide cover for them. Shayan sprints to the ditch to relay orders. The ANA soldiers refuse. One of them is sure that there are IEDs in the road. The whole time, 50-caliber bullets are flying.

Shayan runs back to Bell and reports what the ANA soldiers have told him. Shayan then offers to drive one of ANA vehicles and lead the way back. The look of steely calm in his face leaves no question that he can and will do it if ordered. But they are here to train the Afghans cowering in the ditch. This ambush is another teachable moment. Shayan's job is to communicate orders to the ANA soldiers. Bell refuses Shayan's offer and tells him that he needs to convince them to get in their trucks because they are about to run out of ammunition. Once they run out of ammo, they will not be able to get the ANA soldiers out safely. Shayan runs back to the Afghan soldiers, all the while getting shot at. He manages to persuade the ANA soldiers to get back in their trucks and move out. Whoever was in the field does not follow them as they head back to Camp Khilagay. Somehow, they all get out without casualties.

This is but one incident that shows Carson that Shayan and the other translators are not just expendable human assets. They are indispensable allies. They embody the idea of selfless service, honor, and integrity that all US soldiers are trained to uphold. Shayan is more than an employee of the US government. He is a brother in arms.

A month before Carson is scheduled to leave, he learns that Pasoon is back. Somehow, Passon managed to get back into the ANA. Carson tries to impress upon the kandak commander that he needs to take this threat seriously. Unfortunately, threats against Shayan are not the commander's highest priority. And Carson's influence has waned. He leaves Shayan in the hands of his successor, hoping for the best.

Four years later

Carson receives a request to support Shayan's application for a Special Immigrant Visa. The Taliban and Pasoon have continued to threaten him because he works for the US government.

Shayan put his life on the line to serve with the US military and other coalition forces. From Carson's recollection, he served with more integrity than some of the US soldiers Carson worked with in Afghanistan. Shayan believed that we could stabilize his country, as we promised we would. Instead, he was forced to flee because of his work with and for the US government. He left behind his mother and sister, hoping they would not be targeted, and went into hiding. The Special Immigrant Visa was created exactly for people like Shayan.

Without hesitation, Carson and Captain Bell write letters in support of Shayan's application. But the process is long and more complicated than it should be.

Shayan's application is eventually denied. As of this writing, as far as we know, he is still on the run from the Taliban and Pasoon.

Chapter 1

Introduction

When Captain Jeffrey Carson deployed to Afghanistan as an intelligence officer with the Ohio National Guard in 2009, he hoped that the months would pass quickly and that he would make it home alive and in one piece. During this deployment, the mission was to work with an embedded training team in remote locations. The goal was to train Afghan National Army service members. It was during this deployment that he learned first-hand how important translators and other local hires, as they are called, are to the US mission in Afghanistan. Carson came to understand how profoundly dangerous their job really is and how much they sacrifice to support our mission. Few in the US understand that translators and other local hires are often viewed as traitors by other Afghans. Local hires put an enormous amount of trust in the US promise to create a new country free of warlords and dictators. And many become targets of insurgents because of that. For those threatened because of their work with and for the US government, Congress created a Special Immigrant Visa (SIV) to evacuate, admit, and resettle them and their immediate family in the United States.[1]

But it was during this deployment that Captain Carson came to understand how difficult it can be to obtain the SIV, even for individuals experiencing a documented and serious threat. He saw how many of our allies were forced to live on the run, sometimes with their entire families, while they waited for the completion of a complex bureaucratic process. This raised questions about the laws and policies that are supposed to enable the admission and resettlement of the foreign nationals who work for the US government in support of US foreign policy and whose lives are threatened because of that relationship.

In this book, we explore the development of the laws and policies enabling the evacuation, admission, and resettlement of foreign nationals across four US military interventions. Specifically, we investigate the statutory basis for evacuation and admission, and the regulatory process in the resettlement. Our case studies focus on the evacuation and resettlement of the South Vietnamese (starting in 1975), Iraqi Kurds (starting in 1996), and the Iraqis and Afghans in our current wars. We also explore the actual experience of admission and

---

[1] Special immigrant visas are created by Congress and tailored to specific groups of people. The various types of special immigrants are defined in Immigration and Naturalization Act, §101(a)(27). The SIV that is the focus of this book applies to foreign nationals who have worked directly with the US Armed Forces or under the Chief of Mission in Afghanistan and Iraq. See Appendix A for more details.

resettlement. Some of this information comes from existing reports from a variety of agencies and organizations. In addition, we conducted interviews with current SIV holders from Afghanistan and Iraq.

Some of the laws and policies have evolved over time. One thing that has not changed is that those resettled in the US are admitted and treated as refugees. Administratively, several aspects of the process are more organized for current Iraqi and Afghan allies than they were for the South Vietnamese and Iraqi Kurds. There is now a specific visa (the SIV) enabling entry of Afghan and Iraqi allies.

However, the admission process to the US today is considerably more complex. Resettlement is also more difficult because refugee resettlement policies have not adjusted to the current economic and socio-cultural context in the US. Current laws, policies, and practices are woefully inadequate to pay back the debt of loyalty to those whose lives are threatened because they put their trust in our promises to rebuild their nations and protect them as our employees.

A little history

Since the US withdrawal from Vietnam in 1975, every person displaced because of their work with and for the US government is admitted to the United States as a refugee. The policies that enabled the mass evacuation, admission, and resettlement of large numbers of foreign nationals goes back to the response to people displaced as a consequence of World War II (WWII).

Displaced Persons Acts

The 1948 Displaced Persons Act (DPA) was the first congressionally authorized refugee program in the United States.[2] The law was necessary in order to overcome one very important barrier to the admission of displaced persons: the nation based immigration quotas. These racist quotas were created specifically to restrict migration from Southern and Eastern Europe. However, because the quotas were strictly enforced, they prevented the admission of many of those who became displaced after the war. It was originally supposed to be a two year program but was extended and modestly expanded once by the 1950 DPA. Between 1948 and 1952, the DPA provided a path to entry for displaced persons outside the quotas.

The DPA was the source of anxiety for many nativist members of Congress. Anti-immigrant legislators argued that the law would enable "hordes" of undesirables to enter the US. Many of these undesirables included Eastern and Southern Europeans and Jews. They also warned

---

[2] Daniels, R. (2005). *Guarding the golden door: American immigration policy and immigrants since 1882.* New York, NY: Hill & Wang.; Genizi, H. (1993). *America's fair share: The admission and resettlement of displaced persons, 1945-1952.* Detroit, MI: Wayne State University Press; Reimers, D. M. (1983). An unintended reform: The 1965 Immigration Act and third world immigration to the United States. *Journal of American Ethnic History,* 3(1), 9-28.

that non-Europeans would seek to migrate to the US under these laws. However, few members of Congress believed that the DPA would apply to those outside of Europe and on this, at least, they were proven correct.[3]

The implementation of the DPA created the first refugee resettlement agency: The Displaced Persons Commission (DPC). The DPC developed policies and practices that are still part of the current refugee admission and resettlement process. First, security clearances became a regular part of the admissions review process. In the post-WWII/ early Cold War period, this was largely focused on ensuring that communist agents pretending to be displaced persons would be prevented from entering the US. One important consequence of this is that it extended the review process. It took an average of 8-9 months to process all of the paperwork to approve the admission of a displaced person. Moreover, the security vetting process established a culture of suspicion of all applicants.[4]

Another aspect of refugee admission inherited from the DPC is the requirement that refugees have sponsors and that those sponsors provide housing and job guarantees.[5] There were two types of sponsors that the DPC allowed. The first were individual hosts willing to

---

[3] Reimers, *An unintended reform*
[4] Genizi, *America's fair share*
[5] Daniels, *Guarding the golden door*

provide housing and a job. The second were non-profit or religiously affiliated voluntary agencies that provided blanket assurances of housing and jobs in a particular area without specifying the details of either. The first was preferred by the DPC but the latter became the primary way in which refugees ended up being admitted and resettled.[6]

Congress has historically been preoccupied with immigrants becoming a public charge (i.e., dependent on government assistance). This is reflected in the DPA's focus on the employment of refugees. In particular, the statute emphasizes placing displaced persons in agricultural labor. This led to many problems in practice. The emphasis on farm work resulted in the inappropriate placement of some displaced persons to jobs they were not skilled or suited for. Many refugees, even those coming from rural areas, were not accustomed to particularities of the US agricultural labor market. Displaced persons who were sponsored by Southern farmers were made sharecroppers, which most refugees found unacceptable. Many simply left the farms and headed to cities where they could be among co-ethnics.[7]

There were other problems with the implementation of the DPA.

---

[6] Genizi, *America's fair share.* The practice of cooperating with voluntary agencies in the resettlement of displaced persons did not start with the DPA or DPC. President Truman initiated the practice in order to get around the public charge exclusion criteria in then-existing immigration law. The 1948 DPA was the first time that Congress codified the practice. See also Daniels, *Guarding the golden door.*
[7] Ibid

Chief among them was that some local agencies gave assurances that they could not deliver on. There were frequent reports of displaced persons arriving at their destination with no sponsor to meet them, making them homeless and unemployed upon arrival. In addition, the security clearances, while lengthy, were not infrequently less than vigorous. As a result, Nazi war criminals were able to take advantage of the program and enter the US in direct contradiction to the law.[8]

One of the bright spots in the implementation of the DPA was the creation of state level Displaced Persons Commissions/ Committees in 36 states. In 22 states, state legislators also appropriated funding to these commissions.[9] The state Displaced Person Commissions/ Committees were a very important part in the success of the DPA. They were effective at collaborating with the voluntary agencies and organizing groups at the local level to welcome and support the settlement of displaced people.[10]

Nevertheless, inadequate resources, ambiguous policy direction from the statutes, and the challenge in creating an organizational structure straddling the US and Europe made the process of admitting refugees difficult. Intimidation by anti-immigrant members of Congress also did not help.[11] However, the DPA enabled over 400,000

---

[8] Ibid
[9] Daniels, *Guarding the golden door*
[10] Genizi, *America's fair share*
[11] Ibid

refugees to enter the US in excess of the immigration quotas.[12] Most importantly, it established the practice of offering safe haven for persecuted peoples and set many precedents for future refugee admission and resettlement.

McCarran-Walter Act of 1952

Officially the Immigration and Nationality Act (INA), this law consolidated the various statutes regulating immigration and naturalization. One of its most important provisions was getting rid of the racist nation-based quotas, replacing them with hemispheric limits instead. It also codified family reunification as the main consideration for admission. Of particular importance in this study is the parole authority the law grants to the president. The law gave the executive branch the authority to grant temporary admission to foreign nationals for emergency reasons or when the president determined it was in the public's interest.[13]

The first president to assert the use of parole authority was President Franklin Delano Roosevelt who ordered that some displaced people in Europe be brought to the US and sent to refugee camps at military bases. They were expected to return to their home countries after the war ended. Roosevelt's assertion of parole authority had no

---

[12] Reimers, *An unintended reform*
[13] Daniels, *Guarding the golden door*

8

congressional authorization.[14]

President Eisenhower was the first president to use statutorily granted parole authority and he set an important precedent in doing so. The parole authority was envisioned as something to be used in an emergency for individuals. However, in the first use of the parole authority, Eisenhower granted parole to all Hungarians displaced by the USSR's violent suppression of the Hungarian revolution. In short, Eisenhower used the parole authority for an entire class of immigrants, not just for individuals.[15]

The INA was amended by the Immigration and Nationality Act of 1965. This law did not change the parole authority provided in the 1952 INA. However, in the hearings leading up to the passage of the 1965 statute, Congress made clear that because it was providing a quota for refugees in the law, they expected the president to use parole authority less. The hearing reports also explicitly state that the intent of Congress is that parole authority be used on an emergency basis and only for individuals, not for whole classes of people. However, on the very same day President Johnson signed the 1965 law, he ignored the will of Congress and publicly stated his intent to parole all refugees

---

[14] Ibid. Unsurprisingly, many of those brought in under this program ended up being resettled in the US.
[15] Reimers, *An unintended reform*

fleeing Cuba.[16]

Other laws

Congress repeatedly passed laws to admit displaced persons outside of existing quotas. In addition to the previously described statutes, there was also the Refugee Relief Act of 1953. This law added 200,000 refugees on top of the existing quotas. It also, for the first time, included quotas for some Asians as well as people we would today call Middle Easterners. The 1960 Fair Share Law permitted additional European refugees to enter in order to contribute to UN goals of closing European refugee camps.[17] The 1980 Refugee Act increased the limit for refugees to 50,000 per year.[18] In this statute, Congress also authorized the president to increase the cap for a period of one year if an "emergency refugee situation exists."[19]

None of these laws envisioned the situation in Vietnam, Iraqi-Kurdistan, Iraq, or Afghanistan. Non-Europeans were not even a relevant consideration when the 1948 DPA was passed. Displaced Europeans were also the main humanitarian concern when Congress authorized parole authority to admit and resettle refugees in 1952. As presidents continued to use their parole authority in response to the

---

[16] Ibid
[17] Ibid
[18] Daniels, *Guarding the golden door*; Reimers, *An unintended reform*
[19] Refugee Act of 1980, Public Law 96-212 §207(b)

United States' ever changing foreign policy, most of it involving regions outside of Europe, later laws attempted to provide congressional authority to existing practice and regulate the process in some way.

What do the laws and policies look like today?

The resettlement of foreign nationals occurs under the legal authority granted by the 1965 amendments to the INA as well as through amendments made in the 1980 Refugee Act. The INA establishes the admission criteria for foreign nationals through the asylum, refugee, and SIV categories. The INA details the eligibility criteria for assistance with resettlement. It also authorizes federal assistance programs to support resettlement and facilitate the goal of economic self-sufficiency within one year of arrival.

Immigration and Nationality Act

The resettlement of SIV holders is authorized in the Immigration and Nationality Act (INA) Title IV Chapter 2 Sec.411-414. These provisions in the INA authorize federal assistance programs for refugees through the Office of Refugee Resettlement (ORR) in the Department of Health and Human Services. In coordination with the U.S. Department of State, Congress authorizes ORR to receive funding, coordinate with federal and non-governmental agencies, and establish grants for resettlement programs. It authorizes the provision of financial and medical assistance to refugees. It also requires equality in the distribution of benefits to men and women.

Like the DPA, economic self-sufficiency is the primary goal of refugee resettlement. Economic self-sufficiency is described as being "free from long term dependence on public assistance" and it is explicitly viewed as a matter of employment.[20] Refugee assistance programs are to prioritize employment services and training. Even social service funding should focus on employment related services. English language training is explicitly encouraged but also second to employment, as seen in the provision that English language instruction is to take place during "non-work hours where possible."[21]

Eligibility for financial assistance is predicated in part on active participation in jobs programs and accepting employment determined to be appropriate by the refugee resettlement agency. Refugees are required to participate in any employment programs determined to be appropriate by the state agency, go to any job interviews arranged by the state agency, and accept any offer of employment determined to be appropriate by the state agency. Any employable refugee who refuses or fails to go to a job interview, refuses or fails to accept a job offer, or quits "without good cause" can lose eligibility for financial

---

[20] Immigration and Naturalization Act, §412(a)(2)(C)(iii)(III)
[21] Immigration and Naturalization Act, §412(a)(1)(B)(ii)

assistance.[22]

Voluntary agencies serve a crucial role in the resettlement, as they have since WWII. The INA effectively grants agencies outside of the federal government with authority and responsibility for refugee resettlement. ORR coordinates with volunteer agencies and state and local governments to ensure placement of refugees in areas where employment opportunities, as well as affordable housing and other resources (e.g., education and health care), are available. Unlike previous practice, the INA discourages the placement of refugees in areas "highly impacted ... by presence of refugees or comparable populations" except for the purpose of family reunification.[23]

The INA details the required reports that ORR must submit and on what basis. In line with the goal of economic self-sufficiency, reports to Congress are required to contain labor force statistics of resettled immigrants, the numbers of refugees that are "[s]ignificantly and disproportionately dependent on welfare," the broad geographical location of refugees, and how ORR will improve achievement of the goal of "self-sufficiency."

---

[22] Immigration and Naturalization Act, §412(e)(2)(A)
[23] Immigration and Naturalization Act, §412(a)(2)(C)(i)

Office of Refugee Resettlement Regulations

ORR regulations are found in Title 45 CFR §400.[24] Consistent with the INA, the regulations assume that employment is what will lead to economic self-sufficiency. Economic self-sufficiency is defined in the regulations as enabling an individual family to "support itself without cash assistance grants." The regulations specifically aim to achieve employment within one year of entry, as dictated in the INA.

Financial and medical assistance operates in coordination with existing social welfare assistance programs, specifically Temporary Aid to Needy Families (TANF), Supplemental Security Income (SSI), and Medicaid. The regulations prohibit states from providing less assistance than what is offered to other eligible participants in these programs. They also require that refugees be eligible for Medicaid and SCHIP. However, states are not required to provide financial or medical assistance to full time college or graduate students. Federal assistance for refugees participating in these programs ends after 36 months.

ORR regulations require that state and local refugee settlement agencies provide notices, policies, and other information to refugees in their primary language. These communications should be in writing for

---

[24] 45 CFR §400 can be found at https://www.ecfr.gov/cgi-bin/text-idx?SID=cc2a4e2d54c58f2561aa871d3fb72824&mc=true&node=pt45.2.400&rgn=div5

the major non-English language groups in the specific state but make no explicit provision for the real possibility of illiteracy in the refugee's native language. Alternative methods of ensuring effective communication, including verbal translation, are required only for language groups that exist in smaller numbers in the given state.

State and local resettlement agencies are also required to coordinate with mutual assistance associations (MAAs) or other organizations that represent or serve ethnic groups being resettled. The explicit purpose of this requirement is to ensure that the services provided address the linguistic and cultural needs of refugees and to coordinate with the longer term services provided by MAAs and similar groups.

Consistent with INA, ORR prioritizes services that lead to employment of "employable" family members. This includes wives regardless of employment history or whether there are children in the family. Employable is defined by each state or local resettlement agency in its refugee resettlement plan. As mandated in INA, refugees are required to participate in any jobs program, go to any job interview, and accept any employment offer determined to be appropriate by the state or local agency. ORR regulations state that offers of employment must be accepted without regard to whether the offer is for temporary or permanent work, and regardless of whether it is for full time or part time or even seasonal work. Employment must be accepted even if the job will disrupt participation in other support or social services, including English language training.

Refugees are not required to work in places that violate health and safety laws, where the commute is more than 2 hours or longer than generally accepted for the area, pays less than minimum wage, where the job is essentially a strikebreaking position, or where taking the job would otherwise violate union rules.

English language instruction is also a priority in funding, consistent with the INA. The regulations state that English language training be focused on obtaining and retaining employment. The regulations prohibit sequential language and employment training. In other words, a refugee's family self-sufficiency or individual employability plan cannot be structured to learn English first and then look for a job. Employment is always the priority.

While support to obtain employment is prioritized, the regulations explicitly exclude training that lasts for more than one year. Professional refresher or recertification assistance for refugees with professional training and certification is available as long as it does not take more than one year to complete. These services are only available to refugees who are already employed.

Refugee Resettlement in Action

Despite important constraints on supporting evacuation and resettlement, there is flexibility in the language of the INA and associated regulations that allows Congress and the President to tailor that assistance to the particular conflict.[25] While there has been little consistency in the operations of these programs, the one common thread is the use of the existing refugee resettlement infrastructure.[26]

The general process of SIV admission and resettlement appears deceptively simple. The first part of the process involves extensive background checks. There is also additional processing required to determine eligibility for refugee status and assistance. Those foreign nationals who successfully complete these processes will be granted permission to travel to the US with their eligible family members.

---

[25] Different conflicts used different categories to facilitate entry. Refugee status was the category authorized in the evacuation of South Vietnam following the collapse of Saigon. Under the INA, refugee status can be given to an individual who is outside of his/her country and is unable or unwilling to return because of persecution or fear of persecution on account of race, religion, nationality, or membership in a particular political or social group. In contrast, asylum status was used in the Kurdish Iraqi evacuation. Asylees are defined as foreign nationals already in the US who have established the claim of refugee under the INA. The Special Immigrant Visa (SIV) was authorized by Congress beginning in 2006 to evacuate and resettle Afghans and Iraqis in the current wars.
[26] In general, resettlement assistance operates on a one-size fits all model. Interestingly, Cuban refugees are the one exception to this pattern. Cuban refugees were provided with more and different assistance in retraining and employment recertification than any other refugee group before or since. See Daniels, *Guarding the golden door*.

Once they arrive, they are eligible for the same assistance available to all other immigrant and refugee visa holders, including the ability to adjust their status to Legal Permanent Resident after one year of residency. This simple outline belies that complex processes and organizations that historically have been and currently are involved in the process of evacuating and resettling foreign nationals who work for the US government and become displaced because of that relationship.

What did we find?

The resettlement of foreign nationals who sacrifice for the US in a conflict zone and become targeted because of that relationship is a little known but very important foreign policy tool for the United States. The opportunity to resettle allies helps with recruiting future allies in those places. It creates and maintains a credible reputation of taking care of allies who become threatened because of their support for US military missions.

Currently, the US government has no consistent admission or resettlement policy for foreign nationals who work for and with the US government and are then displaced under threat or targeted due to that relationship. Congress and the President decide funding, admission levels, resettlement, and organizational processes on a conflict-by-conflict basis.

We find that the process of evacuation, admission, and resettlement for the South Vietnamese and Iraqi Kurds was far more successful than it has been for current SIV holders from Afghanistan and Iraq. Part of the reason for this is the varying political, economic, and socio-cultural context of each case. Another reason is that the current resettlement policies do not adequately address the needs of Afghan or Iraqi SIV holders given the present economic and socio-cultural context.

Achieving self-sufficiency is incredibly difficult especially given the emphasis on quickly finding employment with little to no regard to the skills or potential of the SIV holder. The placement of SIV holders generally disregards their transportation needs or the accessibility or adequacy of medical and mental health services. We encountered stories of SIV holders feeling compelled to enter the unpredictable gig economy or being made homeless because of an agency's poor administration. Some SIV holders gave up on the US and returned to their home country, with the worst of all possible outcomes in one case.

Unlike in previous resettlements of this type, SIV holders often have little choice about where they are placed. The effectively random placement of SIV holders and lack of attention to the social and cultural needs of SIV holders is one of cruelest aspects of current policy. Socially and culturally, anti-immigrant attitudes have reached levels the US hasn't seen since the early 20th century. Religious bias against Muslims rivals the shameful history of anti-Semitism and even anti-Catholicism in the US. Fomenting anti-immigrant and anti-Muslim bias is politically expedient in the current era as well. The policy of dispersing SIV holders across the country ignores the dangers of social isolation in a country that is increasingly hostile to Muslim immigrants.

SIV holders deserve more than the inadequate assistance they are provided as refugees. They come to the US believing our promises only to find themselves hindered in their ability to become financially self-sufficient or to contribute to the communities they are placed in. This is offensive to any sense of honor given the risks and sacrifice made by our allies. It is also counterproductive to the US mission.

As of this writing, the US is going to be in Iraq and Afghanistan for the foreseeable future. There will be other conflicts where we will need to make good on our pledge to protect foreign nationals who work with the US in support of our foreign policies. For current and future SIV holders, it is imperative that the process from evacuation to resettlement be as smooth as possible. Our laws and policies also need to be structured to enable successful integration economically and socially. We make several recommendations to strengthen the entire process from evacuation to resettlement. Our aim is to improve current laws and policies so that our promises can be trusted and we maintain the kind of integrity worthy of the selfless service made by our allies.

PART I

HISTORY OF ADMISSION AND RESETTLEMENT OF US ALLIES

The approach to resettling foreign nationals whose lives were threatened because of their relationship to the US has been tested, on a large scale, four times in our nation's history: Vietnam (1975), Iraqi Kurds (1997), Iraq (2006) and Afghanistan (2006) To evaluate the four large scale resettlements, of foreign nationals who worked for and on behalf of US forces, this chapter will present each event be describing the politics, the evacuation, the arrival, and the resettlement in the US.

Chapter 2 will describe the history of the evacuation, admission, and resettlement of the South Vietnamese and Iraqi Kurds. Chapter 3 will describe the admission and resettlement process for Afghan and Iraqis starting in 2006.

Chapter 2

Vietnam and Iraqi Kurdistan

❖ ❖ ❖ ❖ ❖

Vietnam

The depth and breadth of the US government involvement in Vietnam rivaled the US government involvement in Europe during and after World War II. The decisions made by all administrations were based on the National Security Council (NSC) conclusion that Indochina, and more specifically Vietnam, were vital to our national interests.[1] Foreign policy decision-making at that time was based on the "domino theory," which asserted that if one nation in Southeast Asia fell to communism then the entire region could crumble. This belief led five administrations to mobilize millions of troops and spend billions of dollars.[2]

The US involvement with Vietnam and Indochina began in 1950 with President Harry Truman and his administration's support of the colonial power France. The French military were stretched thin

---

[1] National Security Council. (n.d.). *National Security Council*. Retrieved January 15, 2015, from http://www.whitehouse.gov/administration/eop/nsc/
[2] Kissinger, H. (2003). *Ending the Vietnam War: A history of America's involvement in and extrication from the Vietnam War*. New York: Simon & Schuster.

following WWII and suffered huge losses in guerilla fighting with the Vietnamese. Their withdrawal left a vacuum that the Eisenhower administration filled with financial support and military advisors.[3]

The Kennedy administration ramped up the advisor role and, for the first time, US interest in the country became vested in not only winning the tactical military war but also in nation building and changing the political culture. The Johnson administration was under political pressure from Republican realists to do more and was also motivated to compromise in order to push the "Great Society" legislation through Congress. As a result, he further increased the US military and diplomatic involvement in the region. Nixon, however, campaigned on withdrawing with dignity from Vietnam and, once elected, began the withdrawal of troops.

The US government was heavily invested in the health, welfare, and success of the South Vietnamese government. Quantitatively, the US was in Vietnam from the mid-1950s to April 1975 and the US military troop presence reached 500,000 at its height. Qualitatively, the Vietnamese economy, political system, and security system was increasingly dependent on the US government over this time.[4]

The world remembers United States' long and costly war with

---

[3] Ibid
[4] Hein, J. (1995). *From Vietnam, Laos, and Cambodia: A refugee experience in the United States*. New York: Twayne.

Vietnam and its denouement: the hasty withdrawal from the Saigon
Embassy. The collapse of Saigon and the large scale waves of
immigrants required far more economic and social assistance than US
had been prepared for. In 1975, the North Vietnamese Army (NVA)
overran the US-backed South Vietnamese Army and ended what was
25 years of a failed US foreign policy in the region. For the first time,
the US military's use of force was rebuffed and policymakers were left
to consider what to do with foreign nationals who worked for and with
the US government and were now targeted due to that relationship.[5]
The indecision and debate about the South Vietnamese, after the fall of
Saigon, would further damage the United States.

Throughout the US involvement in Vietnam, no policy was ever
developed to assist the South Vietnamese nationals if the country
collapsed and were overrun by North Vietnamese forces. After the fall
of Saigon and the US capitulation in Vietnam, Congress debated, along
with the US public, what to do with an estimated one million
Vietnamese and their family members who had worked for and with
the US government.[6]

Policymakers at all levels of the government and military had no
playbook or lessons learned from past conflicts to help manage an

[5] Kissinger, *Ending the Vietnam War*
[6] Ibid

evacuation of this magnitude.[7] With only weeks before the fall of Saigon, the Ford administration was left with the incredible responsibility of creating and enacting a policy for Vietnamese allies who would be targeted after the fall of Saigon. A creative interpretation of the Immigration and Naturalization Act (INA) allowed the administration to accept an initial 130,000 Vietnamese under the parole status.[8]

To legally operate and administer the incoming Vietnamese immigrants, the administration established an Interagency Task Force (IATF) of 12 federal government agencies. The task force would be responsible for accepting the fleeing South Vietnamese and ultimately resettlement in the US.[9] Although the Indochinese Refugee Program and IATF's broader mission included immigrants from Laos and Cambodia, the majority of parolees processed and resettled in the US were Vietnamese.[10]

Defining the Vietnamese who fled South Vietnam before the fall of Saigon as refugees is somewhat complicated and murky. According to the United Nations Refugee Agency, a refugee, as defined by the 1951 United Nations Convention, is "someone who is unable or unwilling to

---

[7] Ibid
[8] Marsh, R. E. (1980). Socioeconomic status of Indochinese refugees in the United States: Progress and problems. *Social Security Bulletin*, 43(10), 11-20.
[9] Marsh, *Socioeconomic status of Indochinese refugees in the United States*
[10] Scanlan, J., & Loescher, G. (1985). *Calculated Kindness*. New York, NY: The Free Press.

return to their country of origin owing to a well-founded fear of being persecuted for reasons of race, religion, nationality, membership of a particular social group, or political opinion."[11] In April of 1975, the Vietnamese allies who were air-evacuated from South Vietnam were not displaced in another country. Also, the fear of their persecution by the North Vietnamese was presumptive. The US policymakers created a refugee group by evacuating the South Vietnamese because the alternative appeared to be persecution by the North Vietnamese. The experience in Vietnam serves as the starting point for all policy and decisions regarding the withdrawal and resettlement of US allies in future conflicts.

The Politics

The political fault lines of the war, party politics, or immigration were not necessarily evident in the decision to assist South Vietnamese allies in the weeks prior to the fall of Saigon. Because many US Americans viewed Vietnam as a proxy war against Russia and communism, the primary concern amongst policymakers centered on the United States' ability to project power in the face of a defeat. When Vietnam began to crumble and the question of Vietnamese immigrants arose, US policymakers from both parties quickly agreed on the

---

[11] United Nations High Commissioner for Refugees. (2012, August 02). *UNHCR global resettlement statistical report*. Retrieved from http://www.unhcr.org/52693bd09.html.

urgency to support our allies in the region. Albeit very late in the game, policy making, financial appropriation, and advocacy moved forward with some urgency.[12]

One could argue that the US had a responsibility to aid and assist the waves of Vietnamese fleeing potential persecution. The first two waves represented, or at least were designed to represent, those Vietnamese who worked for and with the US forces and would be targeted because of that relationship. President Ford gave multiple speeches leading up to the evacuation of Saigon. In those speeches, he continually uses the term *"moral obligation"* to describe our debt to those who worked for and with the US.[13]

There were also political considerations. Neither President Ford nor Congress were interested in allowing thousands of allies in Vietnam to be tortured, imprisoned, or killed on television because of their alliance with the US.[14] Ford's executive action along with Congress' support injected compassion, heroism, and humanity into an otherwise-depressing narrative.

With little time to act through Congress or to allow the Department of State and the former Immigration and Naturalization Services to

---

[12] Scanlan & Loescher, *Calculated Kindness*; Kissinger, *Ending the Vietnam War*
[13] Sahara, A. (2009). *Operations new life/arrivals: U.S. national project to forget the Vietnam War.* Unpublished Masters Thesis, University of California at San Diego. Retrieved from https://escholarship.org/uc/item/8782s7bc
[14] Scanlan & Loescher, *Calculated Kindness*

formulate an immigration policy, the Ford administration took a chapter from past humanitarian crises in Cuba, Hungary, and Haiti to exercise parole status. A policy option originating in the Immigration and Naturalization Act of 1952, parole status may be granted to *"anyone applying for admission into the United States based on urgent humanitarian reasons or if there is a significant public benefit, or for a period of time that corresponds with the length of the emergency or humanitarian situation."*[15] The Ford administration interpretation of the INA allowed him to use parole status to evacuate Vietnamese allies.

The IATF was created on April 18, 1975 and directed by the Department of State. It developed and administered Operation New Life and New Arrival, which was a groundbreaking fusion of 12 US government agencies tasked to accept US-sponsored Vietnamese immigrants and provide safe passage to a relocation center, with the final objective of placement with a US family and resettlement in the US.[16] In 1975, Congress appropriated $405 million for the operation of

---

[15] US Citizenship and Immigration Services. (n.d.). *What is humanitarian parole and how does it apply to asylum seekers?* Retrieved from https://my.uscis.gov/helpcenter/article/what-is-humanitarian-parole-and-how-does-it-apply-to-asylum-seekers

[16] Members of the IATF included Departments of State; Defense; Justice; Health, Education, and Welfare; Transportation; Treasury; Labor; Interior; and Housing and Urban Development, plus representatives of the US Agency for International Development; the US Information Agency; the Central Intelligence Agency; the Office of Management and Budget; and the Immigration and Naturalization

New Life/New Arrival.[17]

With the Department of Justice's approval to waive visa
restrictions and grant parole status for up to 130,000 Vietnamese, the
final evacuation of the 6,000 US citizens began on April 21, 1975. The
visa waiver legally granted parole status to Vietnamese foreign
nationals selected by the US government to resettle in the US.[18] In
1977, Congress passed Public Law 95-145 which allowed those
Vietnamese who were granted parole status to change status and apply
for legal permanent residency after residing in the US for two years.
The law also expedited citizenship for all Vietnamese who entered the
US under the status of parole.[19]

The Evacuation

Saigon collapsed on April 29, 1975. The first high-level
conversations and planning about the evacuation of US personnel or
the South Vietnamese people did not begin until April 8, 1975. Several
factors contributed to the hasty planning. The intelligence estimates of
the South Vietnamese military and attack planning of the North
Vietnamese were miscalculated. The US intelligence estimates were

---

Service. US Department of Defense. (1977). *Operation New Life/New Arrivals:
US Army support to the Indochinese refugee program.*
[17] These appropriations were passed in Public Law 94-23. US Department of
Defense, *Operation New Life/New Arrivals.*
[18] Kissinger, *Ending the Vietnam War*
[19] Marsh, *Socioeconomic status of Indochinese refugees in the United States*

approximately one to two years behind the actual planning and operational ambition of the North Vietnamese.[20]

Complicating matters, President Ford and his administration were lobbying Congress for an additional spending bill of $722 million dollars that would have resupplied the Vietnamese military and stabilized the economy. The administration believed that planning for withdrawal of the US embassy or the military would inevitably sink the spending bill. Because of this, any evacuation planning at the embassy or in Washington was completely forbidden.[21] In addition, the US ambassador in Saigon, Graham Martin, believed that the creation of evacuation planning groups would have sparked panic in the streets of South Vietnam.[22]

Once the Ford administration accepted that no more aid for the South Vietnamese government from Congress was forthcoming, Operation Frequent Wind was launched. Operation Frequent Wind would serve as the authorization to begin withdrawing from South Vietnam and transporting South Vietnamese allies. The administration's action set in motion around the clock flights, buses, boats, and helicopters to withdraw and evacuate. At the US' request, and through diplomatic channels with Russia, the North Vietnamese

---

[20] Kissinger, *Ending the Vietnam War*
[21] Ibid
[22] Snepp, F. (2002). *Decent interval: An insider's account of Saigon's indecent end*. New York: Random House.

allowed safe passage and evacuation for the Americans. Planners capitalized on the window for safe passage and included South Vietnamese allies in the hasty evacuation effort.[23] Massive cargo and transport planes flew around the clock for 10 days. Approximately 65,000 Vietnamese were transported by air and boat out of the country. An additional 65,000 Vietnamese left without US government assistance.[24]

The evacuation of Vietnamese immigrants was far from orderly. With only days before the overthrow of Saigon, Vietnamese immigrants could not depend on flights alone to exit the country. One Vietnamese immigrant stated that during his evacuation by boat, the engine broke down. Fortunately, the boat was met by a US Navy ship. Mechanics from the US attempted to fix the boat, were unable to, and permitted the Vietnamese to board the ship.[25]

Realizing that Vietnamese would also attempt to evacuate by boat, the US Navy served as mid-level transportation. Whatever Navy ships happened to be in the region became temporary holding areas for Vietnamese immigrants. In one account, an immigrant departed on April 29 and was met by the US Navy Ship American Challenger. She stated that the boat's capacity was 1,080 but it eventually picked up

[23] Kissinger, *Ending the Vietnam War*
[24] Scanlan & Loescher, *Calculated Kindness*
[25] Sahara, *Operations new life/arrivals*

7,500 people.[26]

Even the South Vietnamese Navy departed the country using their own military ships. A group of immigrants who departed the country on their own boat saw the Vietnamese Navy at sea, followed the ships for seven days and arrived at Subic Bay, Philippines. The group eventually found their way to Fort Chaffee via Wake Island.[27]

Not everyone escaping was so lucky. According to *"The Vietnamese Experience in America"* by Paul Rutledge, a fourteen year old immigrant described her experience in the hasty withdrawal by boat. While floating out at sea with her family, they were picked up by pirates:

> *I did not know that they were pirates. But one of them grabbed me and forced me onto their boat along with some other girls. Four men took me into the boat and raped me over and over again. I tried to fight them, but they only beat and laughed at me. (p17)*

The evacuation, Operation Frequent Wind, was complimented by Operation New Life which served as the processing of evacuated South Vietnamese using Andersen Air Force Base (AFB) in Guam as the reception center. Due to their proximity and space, Guam and Wake

---

[26] Ibid
[27] Ibid

Island became the primary staging points for all evacuating Vietnamese prior to entering the US. The final phase was Operation New Arrival through which Vietnamese refugees were eventually settled in the United States.

The evacuation of Vietnamese from South Vietnam was both an impressive military operation and a disappointing display of the US government's failure to properly assist foreign nationals who worked for and with the US and would be targeted due to that relationship. From one perspective, the US built an imperfect template for the evacuation of allies following a failed foreign policy. From another perspective, policymakers were negligent in ignoring the possibility of a withdrawal. The lack of a program or policy to properly aid and assist our allies was and will always be remembered as a failure of planning that created a massive humanitarian crisis.

The Arrival

Vietnamese immigrants arrived in three waves. The first wave consisted of those who left Vietnam right before the fall of Saigon (1975). The second wave came immediately following the fall of Saigon (1975-1977). The final phase of Vietnamese immigrants spanned the years 1977-1985 and are known and characterized as

"Boat People."[28]

First Wave. The initial wave of 10,000-17,000 Vietnamese fled as refugees and arrived right before the fall of Saigon. This first wave represented wealthy and educated Vietnamese with marketable skills who were previously connected with US government and business. This group foresaw the downfall of South Vietnam, had the connections and means to evacuate before the fall, and resettled before chaos ensued.

Second Wave. With the initiation of Operation Frequent Wind, the US withdrawal and South Vietnamese evacuation of Vietnam intensified. By the end of April, up to 100,000 Vietnamese passed through the Philippines and the western Pacific by sea or air and were routed to US staging areas to be relocated in the US.[29] Approximately 133,000 Vietnamese immigrants eventually resettled in the US. Of that total, 112,000 Vietnamese refugees were received and processed at Orote Point, Guam. Some Vietnamese flew directly from the Philippines or Wake Island to the resettlement camps at military bases in the US.[30]

---

[28] Schaefer, R. T., & Schaefer, S. L. (1975). Reluctant welcome: U.S. responses to the South Vietnamese refugees. *Journal of Ethnic and Migration Studies*, 4(3), 366-370; Rutledge, P. (1992). *The Vietnamese experience in America.* Bloomington, Ind.: Indiana University Press.
[29] US Department of Defense, *Operation New Life/New Arrivals*
[30] Ibid

While the primary reception and staging center for Vietnamese immigrants was in Guam, the Department of Defense tasked each branch to support reception and resettlement centers domestically as well. The domestic reception centers were located and operated at the Army bases in Fort Chaffee, Arkansas and Fort Indian-Town Gap, Pennsylvania; Marine Corps Base Camp Pendleton, California; and Eglin Air Force Base, Florida.[31] Table 2.1 shows how many Vietnamese immigrants passed through the different military bases as part of Operations New Life/ New Arrival.

Table 2.1: Processing dates and locations for Vietnamese refugees

Location	Dates	Processed
Guam*	23 April 1975 – 24 June 1975	112,000
Fort Chaffee	2 May 1975- 20 December 1975	50,000
Fort Indian-Town Gap	28 May 1975- 15 December 1975	22,000
Eglin/Camp Pendleton	N/A	61,000

Source: US Department of Defense. (1977). *Operation New Life/New Arrivals: US Army support to the Indochinese refugee program*
*Initial site

Third Wave. Once Saigon fell, the South Vietnamese fled by boat, plane, or foot to any other country where they could. Many were in refugee camps throughout the Pacific. With neighboring countries constrained and regime change happening in Cambodia and Laos, some Asian countries began to turn away Indochinese refugees. With a

---

[31] Ibid

growing humanitarian crisis, the US was forced to act. On May 31, 1979, the United Nations Commission for Refugees and the Socialist Republic of Vietnam created the Orderly Departure Program (ODP). The ODP was created because of the unorganized departure of refugees from Indochina and a growing number of countries denying entrance. It was the UN's attempt to regulate the exodus.[32] In the US, the ODP granted Vietnamese asylum seekers refugee status under the Immigration and Nationality Act of 1980.

To qualify for entrance under the ODP, Vietnamese had to fit into one of three categories. Category I represented Vietnamese nationals who were close family members of a US citizens. "Close family member" was defined as spouse, son/daughter, parents, and grandparents. Category II represented Vietnamese who were employed by the US government for a minimum of one year of service after January 1, 1962. Category III represented Vietnamese with ties to the US that are not captured under Category I or II. This is a broad category but importantly includes children of American citizens left in Vietnam and their immediate family members.

The Resettlement in the US

Prior to the resettlement of the first and second wave of

---

[32] Safer, M. (1990). *Flashbacks on returning to Vietnam.* New York, NY: Random House.

Vietnamese, the resettlement system in the US was designed to take in a limited number of refugees at a time. It was not prepared to handle 130,000 at once. Past resettlements consisted of humanitarian resettlement of Hungarians, Cubans, and Haitians. In these cases, the volume of migrants did not remotely match the scale of the South Vietnamese resettlement.

The US policy for receiving and resettling Vietnamese immigrants was to work with state level resettlement groups who receive funding from the federal government for resettlement services. The resettlement agencies provided job training workshops, English language training, cash assistance, and support in navigating the state and federal agencies.

The federal government provided immigrants with a minimum of one year of medical benefits without cost to the family. Despite access to medical care, there were significant challenges and problems for Vietnamese immigrants because of lack of cultural competency in the US medical care system. Southeast Asian medical philosophy differs greatly from Western medicine. Lack of understanding of and ability to work with non-Western cultural belief systems resulted in both medical, and importantly, mental health problems – especially trauma – from being diagnosed and treated.[33]

---

[33] Rutledge, *The Vietnamese experience in America*

Across the three waves of migration, earlier Vietnamese arrivals worked directly with the newly arrived immigrants. Mutual Assistance Associations (MAAs) were established across the US in 1975 which were managed and operated by Vietnamese refugees. They played a crucial role in the integration and adjustment of Vietnamese immigrants into US society. MAAs were affiliated nationally but operated independently and were remarkably successful. MAAs went above and beyond resettlement agencies and served immigrants at a personal level. In some cases, workers would accompany immigrants to the grocery store, arranged driver's training, and provided family reunification services. The MAA's success led to the organization's powerful lobbying effort to members of Congress for better assistance at home and refugee support abroad.[34]

From an employment perspective, the Vietnamese immigrant's adjustment, adaptation, and persistence through any hurdle or obstacle surpassed the US government's expectation of developing self-sufficiency. The economy welcomed the willingness of Vietnamese immigrants to take low wage and low skill jobs. Between 1975 and 1977, less than 5% of Vietnamese heads of households were unemployed in Houston and 6% in Oklahoma City. Some unknown number of immigrants eventually became successful entrepreneurs. There were certainly hurdles. Highly educated Vietnamese were often

---

[34] Ibid

forced to take entry level jobs. Some communities were unresponsive, unwelcome, or even hostile to the perceived infusion of South Asians. Nevertheless, the Vietnamese who were US allies during the Vietnam War and emigrated because of it represent a success story in their arrival and ability to adapt and integrate into society.[35]

In summary

The hasty planning, phased operation, multi-agency processing, and completion of the evacuation of South Vietnamese produced two stories: one embarrassing and the other remarkable.

In one narrative, the US government experienced a colossal foreign policy and military failure. The defeat by the North Vietnamese had a profoundly damaging effect on the US reputation at home and throughout the world. At the most basic level, the US abandoned an ally and poorly planned the evacuation of those Vietnamese who sacrificed and worked for and with the US government. The domestic resettlement agencies and receiving communities were unable to handle the influx of newly arrived immigrants. Resettlement agencies do not operate to serve a specific ethnic group resulting in a lack of cultural competency that was sorely needed given the scale of this resettlement.

In the other narrative, the US evacuated, processed, and resettled

---

[35] Ibid

130,000 Vietnamese immigrants mostly within one year. The establishment of Guam as an initial processing center and the use of domestic military bases for further processing and resettlement was groundbreaking. MAAs filled in the gaps created by domestic resettlement agencies with personal services that addressed the challenges specific to the Vietnamese immigrants.

The South Vietnamese evacuation and resettlement served as a foundation and experience for policymakers moving forward. It was replicated in another mostly successful evacuation and resettlement of our allies in the early 1990s in the aftermath of the first Gulf War.

❖ ❖ ❖ ❖ ❖

Iraqi Kurds

The 1979 overthrow of the US-backed Shah in Iran and subsequent hostage crisis at the US embassy in Tehran left the US embarrassed and seeking retaliation against Iran. With the removal of the Shah, the Ayatollah imposed a form of strict fundamentalist Islam on the country. In the same year, Saddam Hussein, who represented the minority Sunni population, became the newly anointed President of Iraq. He was interested in gaining Western allies to solidify his power. In Cold War fashion, the US backed and provided material support to the Iraqi government to wage a war with Iran.[36] At that time, this alliance between the US and Iraq was in the interest of both countries. From 1982-1989, Iraq and Iran engaged in a bloody war that claimed the lives of millions of citizens. In the end, neither side gained any land or could objectively claim victory.

With aid from the US drying up as the Cold War came to an end in 1991, the Iraq government was faced with a depleted military and a stagnant economy. Part of Iraq's economic problems were rooted in the debt incurred to fund the Iraq-Iran war. This debt resulted in massive loan payments owed to Kuwait, which Kuwait refused to forgive. Hussein's 1989 invasion of Kuwait was aimed at forcing forgiveness of this debt as well as stoking nationalist sentiment in the public. The invasion was a serious miscalculation by Hussein who overestimated his relationship with the West.

Shortly after the invasion, the US led a worldwide UN-backed coalition which ousted the Iraq military from Kuwait and placed heavy sanctions on the Iraq government. The US stopped short of invading Iraq and overthrowing Hussein. However, the US did covertly and overtly support the overthrow of Hussein by providing assistance to the

---

[36] Khadduri, M., & Ghareeb, E. (2001). *War in the Gulf, 1990-91: The Iraq-Kuwait conflict and its implications.* Oxford: Oxford University Press.

Kurds, predominantly located in the north.[37]

In an effort to seize control from Hussein and aid US allies, the UN established safe havens in the north and south of the country. Within the UN safe havens, the Iraqi military was unable to fly or operate military machinery. While the UN coalition was strong and Hussein's military was weak, the safe havens were successful. Over time, however, the oil for food program, which was established to limit Hussein's oil revenue, largely failed in limiting his power. Iraqi leadership was able to circumvent all restrictions placed on the Iraqi government. In addition, while the UN was the face of the operation in northern Iraq, the skeletal presence consisted mostly of US military forces. These forces were there to monitor the no-fly zone, maintain a presence, and establish contacts in the local area. The force structure was minimal, with only several Blackhawk helicopters and no more than a few dozen soldiers. Relatively quickly, UN support to counter Hussein's growing violations in the safe havens weakened.[38]

Unfortunately, ethnic rivalries among the Kurds prevented them from successfully uniting their own region against Hussein. Northern Iraq is dominated by Kurds, who were left without a state following

---

[37] Ibid. The US also provided support to the Shias, predominately located south of Baghdad, to overthrow Saddam Hussein. This book focuses on the US relationship with the Kurds.

[38] Khadduri & Ghareeb, *War in the Gulf, 1990-91*; Johnson, K. W. (2013). *To be a friend is fatal: The fight to save the Iraqis America left behind*. New York: Scribner.

the end of World War II as French and British colonial powers partitioned the region in order to retain control. The Iraqi Kurdish north contains two distinct and extremely divided groups. The Patriotic Union of Kurdistan (PUK) inhabits the northeast of Iraq, has a large land border with Iran, and has typically had good relations with the Iranian government. To the north, the Kurdish Democratic Party (KDP) has a large land border with Turkey and has had a divisive relationship with the Turkish government (see Figure 2.1).

Figure 2.1: Map of Northern Iraq

Source: Kurdish Areas of Northern Iraq (2003). Retrieved from
https://legacy.lib.utexas.edu/maps/middle_east_and_asia/iraq_kurdish_areas_2003.jpg

Our interviewees pointed to the 1996 election as being the tipping
point for Hussein's threats to the north. Around that time, the KDP and
PUK had entered into another civil war against each other. The KDP,
led by Massoud Barzani, was losing ground to the PUK, led by Jalal
Talibani. The PUK was backed by the Iranians. This forced the KDP to
form an alliance with Hussein. Hussein sent troops into the KDP

region and quickly cleared out any PUK presence. There was no international response to his movement into the north.

Interviewees stated that after Hussein sent troops into the north without any reaction from the UN, Hussein announced in several speeches that those working with the UN would be jailed. Hussein never sent troops into Kurdistan but the threat served as a warning to Kurds providing security and logistical support to the UN/US forces enforcing the no-fly zone. Shortly thereafter, foreign troops representing the UN closed bases and began developing an evacuation plan for allies who worked with or on behalf of the UN. While the story did not end well for many Kurdish allies of the US, the 1996 evacuation and resettlement of Iraqi Kurds is an example of the US' ability to help foreign nationals who work for and with the US and are threatened because of that relationship.[39]

The Politics

The use of safe havens from 1991-1996 was a politically safe approach. The foreign policy philosophy of "Domino Theory" that had lead the US to continue the Vietnam War did not apply to Iraq. The fervor and excitement that had gripped the country in the months leading up to and through the Persian Gulf War was nonexistent after the war ended. There was neither a foreign policy objective supporting,

---

[39] Kurdish allies included both KDP and PUK.

nor a domestic constituency lobbying for, keeping UN forces in the north Iraq. In short, Congress and the President had no interest in sending in US troops to deter or fight Hussain.

According to our interviews, the 1996 Iraqi Presidential election was a key factor in President Clinton's decision to evacuate the safe havens and relocate Iraqi Kurds. Even though it was unlikely that Hussein would actually send troops north, President Clinton wanted to avoid a foreign policy crisis during the election. With no military option available, an evacuation of the UN forces was inevitable. The evacuation of Iraqi Kurds was seen as needed to keep any crisis from developing. If Hussein had invaded the north and targeted Iraqi Kurds, the US would have been left in a no-win situation politically. An invasion would either have provoked the US into reacting or, if Clinton chose not to react, the US would have appeared weak. To avoid this entirely, President Clinton ordered the Joint Staff, an organization within the Joint Chiefs of Staff, to develop evacuation options.

While emigrating thousands of Iraqi Kurds during the Iraqi presidential election would be tricky, domestic resettlement posed additional political challenges. According to officials involved in planning the resettlement, sending Iraqi Kurds to the Army Base Fort Indian-Town Gap in Pennsylvania was not politically acceptable. It was a presidential reelection year in the US as well and Clinton's campaign preferred to have no attention paid to this evacuation and resettlement. Once again, Guam would serve the needs of allies who were targeted due to their relationship with the US. The use of Andersen Air Force Base in Guam also had the benefit of minimizing press coverage and unwanted public attention.

The Evacuation

A joint task force, named Operation Pacific Haven, was established to evacuate the Kurdish Iraqis from northern Iraq to be resettled in the US by way of Guam. Very similar to the evacuation of the South Vietnamese, the operation consisted of a combination of government and non-profit agencies, led by the US, and through Andersen Air Force Base in Guam as the processing center.[40]

Operation Pacific Haven was established on September 16, 1996 and lasted 218 days. In total, 6,600 Kurdish evacuees were processed through Andersen Air Force Base with their final destination to be the US. The effort consisted of 1,600 military and interagency personnel. Kurds were provided with medical care, food, housing, and a basic education in language, US customs, and US culture.[41]

In addition to meeting the immediate needs of the newly-arrived refugees, Guam served as a special immigration processing center for the Kurds. The former Immigration and Naturalization Service was

---

[40] The List Project. (n.d.). *Iraq - 1996*. Retrieved from http://thelistproject.org/history/iraq-1996/
[41] Ibid

responsible for processing applicants into the federal immigration database and conducting background checks. The Department of Health and Human Services was responsible for medical screening and matching evacuees with volunteer agencies to be resettled in the US. At that time, a typical asylum process for one person took six months to one year. While on Guam, the interagency task force was able to simplify and expedite the asylum process, shortening the time to three to four months.[42]

According to Lieutenant Colonel Ray Charlesworth, the local community in Guam provided overwhelming support to the Kurdish evacuees. In total, the local Guamanians volunteered over 40,000 hours to support and assist the Kurds and US government. In addition, the US government spent $10 million dollars within the local communities for support and logistical services.[43]

The 1996 evacuation of Iraqi Kurds was remarkably efficient and effective. An important aspect of the experience was the use of Guam as a central location where federal, state, and non-governmental organizations could combine talent and resources to streamline the processing and preparation of these refugees for a future in the US.

---

[42] Ibid

[43] US Department of Defense. (1997, April 15). *Operation Pacific Haven wraps up humanitarian efforts, Release No: 177-97*. Retrieved from http://archive.defense.gov/Releases/Release.aspx?ReleaseID=1218

The Arrival and The Resettlement in the US

Previous Kurdish refugees had settled in Tennessee following the end of the 1990 Gulf war. By 1996, these previous refugees had established roots in the community.[44] The State Department, through resettlement agencies, immediately began coordinating with Tennessee officials to resettle a large portion of the 6,600 Kurds waiting in Guam.

As in the case of South Vietnamese immigrants, an organic support structure within the existing Kurdish community accounted for the successful adjustment and integration of the new arrivals. The State Department and Health and Human Services provided similar resettlement benefits that were afforded to Vietnamese and other refugees in accessing medical services, social assistance, and a path to citizenship. However, the existing Kurdish community members, much like the MMAs, worked at a local and personal level with the arrivals. This grassroots relationship provided the Kurds with a network for employment and social support for integration while maintaining cultural integrity.

The successful integration of the Kurds could be partly attributed to what one state official called "Southern Hospitality." The people of Tennessee had experienced and integrated Kurds into their community

---

[44] Karimi., H. (2010, Feburary 19). The Kurdish immigrant experience and a growing American community. *Kurdish Herald*. Retrieved from: http://ekurd.net/mismas/articles/misc2010/2/kurdsworldwide436.htm

since 1991. So the new arrivals did not pose any new challenges that they were not already prepared for. In addition, Kurds had done a remarkable job in accepting the values and norms of US society.

The successful integration can also be attributed to the affluence and education level of the Kurdish refugees themselves. The Kurdish Iraqis who worked for the US in Iraq were highly educated. They found work in a variety of areas ranging from academia, business ownership, and as civil servants. To some extent, the evacuation was a brain drain of some of the brightest and best citizens in northern Iraq.

In summary

The Kurdish evacuation and resettlement is a little known yet highly successful story. The speed in which the US government developed a course of action, logistically moved, and resettled the Kurds was impressive. Unfortunately, not enough research or published material has been written about this period.

The story of the experiences of evacuating and resettling Iraqi Kurds in 1996 is unfinished. The story told here is from perspective of military personnel involved in the evacuation and resettlement process. The policy story, however, is more complete and one of the few bright spots in the histories of resettling allies threatened because of their relationship with the US. Compared to the evacuation and resettlement of South Vietnamese allies, the policies and procedures used for the

Kurds should be seen as a model for future evacuation and resettlement efforts. As we shall see with the Special Immigrant Visa process of Afghan and Iraq allies in the Global War on Terror, it appears that the US did not look to the lessons that should have been learned in 1996.

Chapter 3

Afghanistan and Iraq

The Global War on Terror (GWOT) or War on Terror was coined by President Bush in the days after the September 11th attacks. The depth and breadth of operations covered under the GWOT span dozens of countries across multiple continents.[1] The focus here is on the US military activities in Iraq and Afghanistan. These conflicts fall under two different operations: Operation Enduring Freedom (as part of the GWOT) and Operation Iraqi Freedom (renamed to Operation New Dawn in 2010). The histories in each place are unique and will be considered separately. As of this writing, these conflicts and the evacuation and resettlement of allies are ongoing processes.

❖ ❖ ❖ ❖ ❖

Afghanistan

During the Cold War, the US and USSR treated small and impoverished countries from Asia through South America like pawns in a global game of chess. The history of the US involvement in Afghanistan specifically dates back to the 1979 Soviet invasion.

---

[1] US Department of Defense. (n.d.). *DoD Authorizes Global War on Terrorism Medals for Operation Freedom's Sentinel.* Retrieved from http://prhome.defense.gov/RFM/MPP/OEPM/Functions

Afghanistan served as one site among many where the two superpowers engaged in proxy wars.

With communism and communist governments on the rise, the ruling government body in the USSR had a special interest in the success of new and fragile communist governments.[2] Through the 1970s and 1980s, the Soviets had successfully squelched democratic uprisings in Hungary and had growing support in France and Italy. The Soviets initially invaded Afghanistan to support a newly formed communist government. This invasion, however, caught US foreign policy experts by surprise.

Initially, the US struggled to effectively respond to the Soviet invasion of Afghanistan. The US and Saudi governments provided funding and military equipment via the Pakistani government. Through the Pakistani intelligence agency, the Afghan mujahideen fighters were equipped with surface to air missiles, automatic rifles, and intelligence. The brutal insurgency campaign resulted in a heavy loss of life for Afghans and Soviets. With Saudi and US support, backed by the Pakistani safe-havens across the border, the Soviet military capitulated in 1989. With the Cold War over, the US pulled funding out of Afghanistan and the country went from a front page topic in global

---

[2] Coll, S. (2004). *Ghost wars: The secret history of the CIA, Afghanistan, and bin Laden, from the Soviet invasion to September 10, 2001*. New York: Penguin Press.

news to a forgotten country.

Following the Soviet withdrawal, the Afghan government collapsed. The mujahideen backed militias no longer had a common enemy. There was also no foreign funding stream to finance the government. With little governance or social progress, it did not take long for civil war to break out. An emerging militia group led by Mullah Omar began to gain momentum in the areas along the Pakistani border that had previously served as safe-havens for foreign fighters and mujahideen. The group, known as the Taliban, imposed adherence to a strict interpretation of the Koran. The Taliban swept through the south and began to unite or destroy local warlords.[3]

As Mullah Omar and the Taliban gained ground in Afghanistan, a disenfranchised Saudi named Osama Bin Laden grew frustrated with the US military presence in the Middle East. Osama Bin Laden had served in Afghanistan and had both funded and worked with the mujahideen. However, upon returning to Saudi Arabia, the government became anxious about his ideology and restricted his travel within the Kingdom.

In response to his disdain for the US and treatment by the Saudi government, Osama Bin Laden founded a global Islamic network whose ideology and foundation was, and still is, the destruction of the

---

[3] Ibid

West, establishment of Sharia law, and liberating all Muslim occupied land. Osama Bin Laden's loosely organized international jihadist organization, Al-Qaeda, arrived in Afghanistan in 1996. Mullah Omar and the Taliban offered Osama Bin Laden safe-haven and a place to train and recruit members of Al-Qaeda.[4] Al-Qaeda's primary target was the US.

There were several bombings in 1998 that were traced to Al-Qaeda but the US did not respond militarily to these attacks. This changed after September 11, 2001. Al-Qaeda hijacked airplanes and crashed them into the World Trade Center and Pentagon. One hijacked flight went down in Pennsylvania. Almost 3,000 people were killed on this date. US policymakers acted swiftly in authorizing a military response. Intelligence traced the funding, training, and leadership of the 9/11 attack to Al-Qaeda and Osama Bin Laden, who explicitly took responsibility for them. As early as October of 2001, units from the US military arrived in Afghanistan.[5]

With the invasion of US and coalition troops, as well as a reestablished diplomatic mission in Afghanistan, the US hired a number of Afghans, known as local hires, to assist the military operations and provide translation, security, and logistical support.

---

[4] Ibid
[5] National Commission on Terrorist Attacks upon the United States. (2004). *The 9/11 Commission report*. Washington, DC. Retrieved from http://govinfo.library.unt.edu/911/report/index.htm

Among the many Afghans who worked for the US government, the interpreter or translators are the primary face of foreign national hires. In 2007, the contract for linguist services in Afghanistan was worth $414 million and was increased to $2 billion by 2012. According to Mission Essential Employees (MEP), a total of 5,816 Afghan linguists were employed on behalf of the US government in just the 2012 contract.[6]

As the security situation weakened in Afghanistan, interpreters became easy targets for insurgents. It also became clear that the US had to have a process for evacuating local hires who could no longer be protected.

> *While my application was being considered, my mother, who lived in Ghazni, died. I wondered if I should go to the funeral, since I knew there were many Taliban operating around my home district. In the end, it was good that I did not, because the Taliban stopped the taxis that were driving to the funeral and asked, "Where is her son, the one who worked for the Americans?"[7]*

[6] Ellison, J. (2015, March 4). *As war nears an end, our Afghan translators are being left behind.* The Daily Beast. Retrieved from http://www.thedailybeast.com/articles/2012/10/21/as-war-nears-an-end-our-afghan-translators-are-being-left-behind.html
[7] Coburn, N., & Sharan, T. (2016). *Out of harm's way? Perspectives of the special immigrant visa program for Afghans.* Hollings Center for International

In 2006, Congress authorized the creation of a new Special Immigrant Visa (SIV) specifically for translators. The implementation was complicated by operational needs as well as bureaucratic inefficiency. As of this writing, the SIV continues to serve as the primary mechanism for protecting allies threatened because of their relationship with the US.

The Politics

From his sanctuary in Afghanistan, Osama Bin Laden issued several fatwas encouraging attacks against the US. The 1998 bombings of the Kobar Towers, USS Cole, and World Trade Center bombings were all backed, to varying degrees, by Al Qaeda and Osama Bin Laden. At the time, the political will in the US to respond militarily was minimal.

Following the 9/11 attacks, however, policymakers and much of the US public were more open to a military response. Congress unanimously passed Public Law 107-40, also known as the Authorization for Use of Military Force (AUMF) two weeks after the attacks. It granted the President the authority to use all "necessary and appropriate force" against those whom he determined "planned, authorized, committed or aided" the September 11th attacks, or who

---

Dialogue. Retrieved from http://www.hollingscenter.org/wp-content/uploads/2016/09/SIV-Full-Report.pdf (p.4)

harbored said persons or groups.[8] In the decade that followed, the authorization has been used to justify and expand operations in Yemen, Somalia, Libya, and Syria, diluting to some extent the original purpose of the AUMF.[9]

Unlike the previous conflicts, the US did not wait until the last convoys scrambled out to create policies and procedures to evacuate and resettle local allies who became threatened because of their relationship with the US. Congress and the Executive branch took time to develop policies and chose to create a new type of SIV for Afghans working for the US in Operation Enduring Freedom. SIV holders are eligible for the same resettlement assistance provided to other refugees. Over time, the legislation authorizing SIVs expanded the eligibility criteria and the numerical caps.

Of the FY2006 National Defense Authorization Act (NDAA), Section 1059 created a visa to both Iraqis and Afghans and are only available to those who have worked directly with the U.S. Armed Forces or under Chief of Mission (COM) authority at U.S. Embassy Baghdad or U.S. Embassy Kabul. Applicants must have worked for the

---

[8] Gropman, A. (2014, Oct 23). *Is the President authorized to attack ISIL?* Retrieved from Military Officers Association of America: http://www.moaa.org/Content/Publications-and-Media/Features-and-Columns/Think-Tank-Nation/Is-the-President-Authorized-to-Attack-ISIL-.aspx
[9] Weed, M. C. (2015, Apr 14). 2001 *Authorization for use of military force: Issues concerning its continued application.* Congressional Research Service. Retrieved from https://fas.org/sgp/crs/natsec/R43983.pdf

US at least one year, demonstrate a serious threat due to their employment and obtain a written letter of recommendation from the Chief of Mission. The numerical cap for in the FY2006 NDAA was 50, not including spouses and children. The cap was increased to 500 in the FY2007 and FY2008 NDAAs.[10]

Beginning in 2009, eligibility for the SIV expanded to include Afghans who had worked for or with the US government in any capacity. In addition, NDAAs for FY2009-2014, and once as separate legislation, continually increased the number of SIVs available. A program that started with a cap of 50 SIVs for translators only in 2006 expanded to 4,000 SIVs for any one working under the Chief of Mission or US Armed Forces in Afghanistan. Importantly, Congress authorized the State Department to carry forward any unused SIVs to future fiscal years. Through the end of 2017, over 15,000 Afghans who have worked for or with the US government and were threatened because of that relationship have been issued a SIV (see Table 3.1).

---

[10] Bruno, A. (2016). *Iraqi and Afghan Special Immigrant Visa programs.* Congressional Research Service. Retrieved from https://fas.org/sgp/crs/homesec/R43725.pdf

Table 3.1: SIV issued to Afghan Translators, Interpreters and Workers for the US

Fiscal Year	Principals	Dependents	Total
2007	95	69	164
2008	401	415	816
2009	282	396	678
2010	35	75	110
2011	37	81	118
2012	117	118	235
2013	678	914	1,592
2014	3,483	5,792	9,275
2015	2,333	4,549	6,882
2016	3,676	8,614	12,290
2017	4,161	12,204	16,365
Total	**15,298**	**33,227**	**48,525**

Source: Bureau of Consular Affairs, US Department of State.

As seen in Table 3.1, Afghan interpreters and employees working on behalf of the US saw relatively quick approvals during the start of the program. From 2007 through 2009, the embassy in Kabul appeared to be issuing in line with the number of visas authorized in the NDAAs. However, the issuance dropped substantially for both interpreters and other employees in 2010 through 2012.[11]

The decline and eventual stagnation of the SIV program at the

---

[11] Bruno, *Iraqi and Afghan Special Immigrant Visa programs*; US Department of State. (n.d.). *Mission*. Retrieved from Bureau of Consular Affairs: https://travel.state.gov/content/travel/en/about-us.html

Kabul embassy is most likely attributed to leadership at the US Department of State. In a February 2010 cable obtained from the Associated Press, then Ambassador Karl Eikenberry wrote to Secretary of State Clinton voicing concern that the SIV program would reduce needed support for the mission in Afghanistan. "This Act could drain this country of our very best civilian and military partners: our Afghan employees." The Ambassador believed that issuance of visas could "have a significant deleterious impact on staffing and morale, as well as undermining our overall mission in Afghanistan. Local staff is not easily replenished in a society at 28 percent literacy."[12]

Eikenberry served as the US Ambassador to Afghanistan from 2009-2011. During that time, the issuance of SIVs dropped 91%. The US embassy left over 4,000 unissued SIVs that were authorized by Congress.

When former Senator John Kerry was appointed Secretary of State, he wrote several Op-Ed articles in support of the SIV program. In June of 2014, Secretary Kerry posted an article in the LA Times writing:

> *The way a country winds down a war in a faraway*
> *place and stands with those who risked their own safety*

---

[12] Sieff, K. (2015, March 09). In Afghanistan, interpreters who helped U.S. in war denied visas; U.S. says they face no threat. *The Washington Post*. Retrieved from http://www.washingtonpost.com/world/in-afghanistan-interpreters-who-helped-us-in-war-denied-visas

to help in the fight sends a message to the world that is
not soon forgotten...As the withdrawal proceeds, the
United States is in danger of sending the wrong
message to Afghan interpreters and others who risked
their lives helping our troops and diplomats do their
jobs in Afghanistan over the last decade.[13]

During Kerry's time as Secretary, the SIV program saw record growth and maximization of SIVs issued. After Ambassador Eikenberry's departure, SIV issuance tripled in 2012 and reached over 4,000 in 2017. This demonstrates how fragile the SIV program is and effect that one Ambassador or Secretary of State can have on the program.

The Evacuation

Several of the Afghan SIV applicants we interviewed stated that their cases were initially rejected because the US Embassy was not convinced that a serious threat existed. According to the Department of Defense (DoD), by virtue of an association with the US government, these interpreters and their family members were clearly in danger of being killed. Even with multiple letters from DoD offices attesting to

---

[13] Kerry, J. (2014, June 2). From John Kerry: We need more visas, now, for our Afghan allies. *Los Angeles Times*. Retrieved from http://www.latimes.com/opinion/op-ed/la-oe-0602-kerry-afghan-withdrawal-20140603-story.html

the threat, the embassy denied interpreters who worked in prisons or conducted numerous raids with Marine units.[14]

In interviews with immigrants and non-profit groups established to support the resettlement of Afghan SIV holders, the Afghan SIV process has severely affected the morale of those applying for the visa. Applicants for the visa live every day under duress and are typically displaced from their family for safety and security purposes. Some families are left to move around the country to avoid detection and all the while depend on the embassy to properly process their application. If they are lucky enough to receive a SIV, the holder and family have a matter of days to sell any possessions, borrow money, and depart Afghanistan. The process, from an Afghan's perspective, is fraught with uncertainty and bureaucracy.

Others have documented similar experiences. Janis Shinwari is one of many faces of a long list of Afghan interpreters and direct employees who have been targeted due to his relationship with the US. Janis served as an interpreter for the US since 2006. Once his identity and relationship with US forces was discovered by the Taliban, he and his family's life became compromised. He routinely received threats by the Taliban and eventually had to move his family every couple days to remain in hiding. After two years of battling with the US bureaucracy and multiple Congressional inquiries on his behalf, Janis

---

[14] Sieff, *In Afghanistan, interpreters who helped U.S. in war denied visas*

and his family were finally issued a Special Immigrant Visa (SIV) to enter the US in 2013.[15]

Participants described a SIV system that was disorganized and unwilling to reform in order to issue the allocated SIVs. For reasons unknown to outsiders, the process continually denied perfectly eligible applicants. Or documents would be misplaced, which delayed the processing of the application. A participant from one non-profit organization described the process as a "leaderless operation." After calls were placed to inquire about an applicant, the State Department was unable to identify where the application was in the process. As described earlier, much of these experiences can be explained by the decisions of an Ambassador concerned about the operational needs of US forces and personnel in Afghanistan. Once a more supportive Secretary of State and new ambassador were appointed, the barriers to issuing SIVs began to come down.

Unlike previous resettlements, Afghan SIV holders are not processed at Andersen Air-Force Base in Guam. Instead, the processing, education, and resettlement details are entirely provided to the SIV holder and family in Kabul. Once this is completed, they depart Kabul International Airport and are flown directly to the United

[15] Packer, G. (2015, March 04). An Afghan interpreter's flight to America. *The New Yorker*. Retrieved from http://www.newyorker.com/news/daily-comment/an-afghan-interpreters-flight-to-america

States.

From interviews, Afghans were typically displaced and had been
on the run throughout Afghanistan before being issued a SIV.
Interviewees reported that there is little time to gather belongings and
put their affairs in order before shipping out. This lack of an
adjustment period is hardly ideal for anyone, especially a family with
children.

The Arrival and The Resettlement in the US

By the end fiscal year 2017, the population of Afghan SIV holders
in the US had increased to almost 50,000. The majority of SIV holders,
and Afghan refugees generally, are settling in five states: California,
Texas, Virginia, Washington, and Maryland (see Table 3.2). These
same three states were also the largest states of resettlement when
looked at relative to the state's population. In short, even when
evaluated relative to a state's population, Afghan SIV holders are
settling in these five states at the high rate (see Figure 3.2).

Table 3.2: Afghan Special Immigrant Visa resettlement by state through FY2017

Alabama	32	Illinois	411	Montana	0	Rhode Island	13
Alaska	0	Indiana	66	Nebraska	334	South Carolina	67
Arizona	641	Iowa	111	Nevada	321	South Dakota	25
Arkansas	19	Kansas	106	New Hampshire	18	Tennessee	277
California	17,791	Kentucky	223	New Jersey	297	Texas	7,184
Colorado	885	Louisiana	43	New Mexico	133	Utah	257
Connecticut	548	Maine	37	New York	1,570	Vermont	2
Delaware	19	Maryland	2,490	North Carolina	545	Virginia	7,025
District of Columbia	18	Massachusetts	311	North Dakota	48	Washington	2,554
Florida	661	Michigan	304	Ohio	414	West Virginia	10
Georgia	925	Minnesota	212	Oklahoma	26	Wisconsin	129
Hawaii	0	Mississippi	3	Oregon	518	Wyoming	0
Idaho	197	Missouri	482	Pennsylvania	621		
						Total	**48,923**

Source: Bureau of Population, Refugees, and Migration, Department of State

Figure 3.1: Afghan SIV resettlement from FY 2007-2017

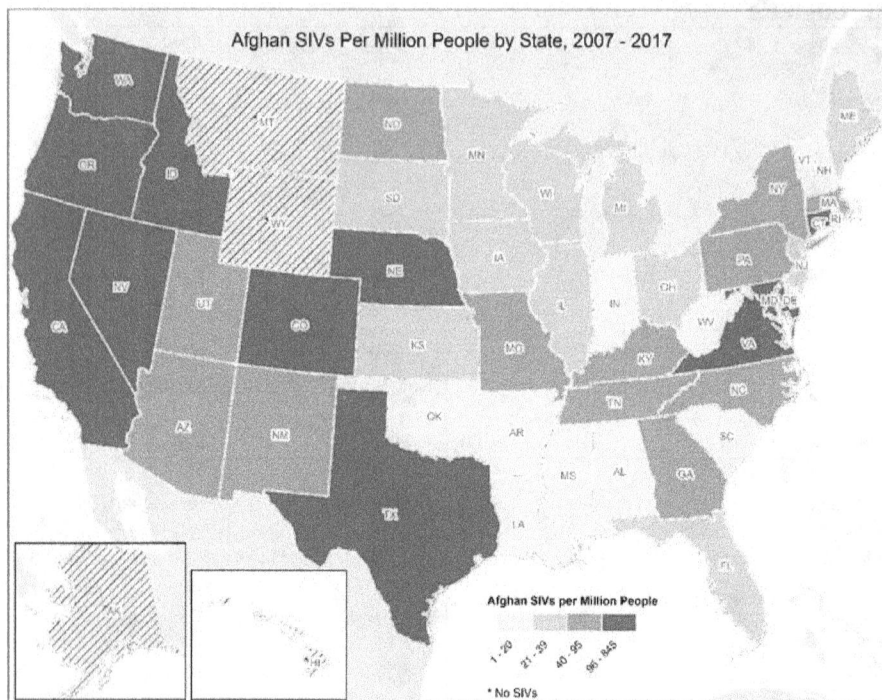

Afghan SIVs Per Million People by State, 2007 - 2017

Afghan SIVs per Million People

1 - 20   21 - 39   40 - 95   96 - 845

* No SIVs

Source: Bureau of Population, Refugees, and Migration. *Admissions & arrivals*. US Department of State.
Retrieved from: http://www.wrapsnet.org/admissions-and-arrivals/

SIV holders are provided the same assistance in resettling as other refugees. However, the resettlement and integration appears to be a much more challenging process than seen with previous resettlements of US allies. Our interviews revealed that Afghans have had a difficult time creating a comfortable space in the US. Afghans lack the social network or a political base to aid and support their adjustment and integration into US society. Afghans are made up of several diverse ethnic groups that rarely had contact with others in Afghanistan. They frequently do not speak the same language. As a society that is primarily based around tribal groups, Afghans do not share the same sense of nationalism seen with Vietnamese and Iraqi Kurd immigrants. This has made it difficult for Afghan refugees to come together for mutual aid and support.

Resettlement groups that work to aid Afghans have argued for better support upon arrival. Afghans are resettled in subpar locations, far from where employment and services are. They are even provided with dilapidated furniture by some resettlement agencies. These groups argue that Afghans who sacrifice for the US are being resettled in abysmal conditions. Afghans are already struggling to exit the country and upon arrival are resettling in substandard conditions with little prospect for success.

In summary

When the Afghan SIV program was put in place, it was structured to succeed. Unfortunately, it was derailed for several years due to the command philosophy of the political leadership. When the command philosophy changed, the program was able to succeed and function in accordance with congressional authorization. However, this case illustrates the fragility of the Afghan SIV program. Congress has debated the authorization of the number SIVs and its eligibility criteria almost every year. Executive agencies perform in accordance with the perspectives of the current appointees. Changes in leadership and political winds create significant uncertainty for the SIV program and the Afghans who risk their lives supporting the US government and military efforts.

Upon arrival, Afghans have not benefited from a networked or social community that aided previous waves of resettled allies from Vietnam or Kurdistan. Further complicating resettlement is the lack of common identity or even common language. Unlike Vietnamese, Kurds, (or, as we shall see, Iraqis), Afghans have not been unified under a national identity. The placement within the country has geographically separated Afghans resulting in very little interaction within or even between ethnic groups. The lack of policies and programs that attend to the unique needs and conditions of Afghans has created unnecessary suffering for these individuals and their families.

❖ ❖ ❖ ❖ ❖

Iraq

President Saddam Hussein had ruled Iraq since the late 1970s and had become an adversary of the US following the invasion of Kuwait in 1991. Over time, and with international attention having moved to events in the former Yugoslavia, he began to chip away at and defy the UN sanctions established following the war. With a robust domestic economy and liberal foreign policy, the Clinton administration was not interested in committing additional military assets or attention to

Iraq.[16] Even with UN sanctions and northern/southern no-fly zones, Hussein's power only grew more lethal. As described earlier, he was able to muscle out UN forces operating in the Kurdish north.

Following the 9/11 attacks and the commencement of the Global War on Terror, Hussein became a target of President George W. Bush. He labeled the Iraqi leader and Iraq itself as a member of the "Axis of Evil" and stated that the war on terrorism had only begun with Afghanistan. For many US Americans, this was a new foreign policy problem.[17]

The case for war in Iraq was vastly different than in Afghanistan. The Bush administration's rationale for war against Iraq depended on its defiance of UN sanctions to forfeit all weapons of mass destruction (WMD). According to the administration's narrative, a defiant and rogue government with WMDs could hold the US and possibly the world hostage to a future attack. Controversially, the administration argued that if Hussein did not comply with the UN sanctions, the US could legally preemptively invade and overthrow the existing leadership.

Conducting this war ended up being more complicated than the arguments for it implied. To begin, no WMDs were ever located and

---

[16] Woodward, B. (2004). *Plan of attack*. New York: Simon & Schuster.
[17] Ibid

several major European countries were never fully invested in the operation. Further, the country's three main ethnic groups (Shia, Sunni, and Kurds) were far more fractured than US policymakers and the Bush administration had envisioned. Finally, the expectation that increased oil output would fund the post war reconstruction turned out to be unrealistic given that Iraq's infrastructure was deteriorated beyond previous estimates.

After the official fall of the Iraqi government on April 9, 2003, the US assumed responsibility for the country's well-being and reconstruction. Unfortunately, it was unable to provide basic services such as water, electricity, or security. Initially, Iraq was governed by the US-led Multi National Force-Iraq (MNF-I). US Ambassador Paul Bremmer III led the Coalition Provincial Authority (CPA). This group was responsible for the immediate leadership, policy, legislation, and basic governing of Iraq.[18] The US became the biggest employer in Iraq. All contracts, rebuilding projects, or work for the government required US approval via the MNF-I and CPA.

The US lacked a full understanding or appreciation of the complex political and cultural reality of Iraq. This contributed to the adoption of policies and approaches that ultimately created the foundation for a

---

[18] Sissons, M., & Al-Saiedi, A. (2013). *A bitter legacy: Lessons of de-Baathification in Iraq*. Washington D.C.: International Center for Transitional Justice. Retrieved from https://www.ictj.org/sites/default/files/ICTJ-Report-Iraq-De-Baathification-2013-ENG.pdf

civil war. Local Iraqis who worked for the US or coalition forces ended up being targeted by a variety of insurgent groups as a result.

The Politics

De-Ba'athification. In Iraq, several political mistakes were made that created the instability that led to the targeting of Iraqis working for US and coalition forces. Arguably the most important of these mistakes was the controversial policy approved by Paul Bremmer called De-Ba'athification. The goal of this policy was to prevent the reemergence of the Baath Party by prohibiting members of the former ruling Baath Party to reenter public service. De-Ba'athification meant that thousands of Iraqis across the government were dismissed. The policy was implemented with little knowledge of the Baath Party hierarchy or Iraqi politics. To work in the government during the Hussein era required allegiance to the Baath Party regardless of personal opinion of Hussein or political preferences. De-Ba'athification left a vacuum that coalition forces were unable to fill. Entire institutions, including the military and security service, as well as civil servants in public institutions, were hollowed out.

For example, $10 million was spent on building a new air traffic control tower in Mosul. The air field was a major hub for flights coming from Turkey and the north. A functioning airport would open commerce and trade, which was important part of rebuilding the country. The tower was completed in 2007, however, it sat empty for years. Coalition forces were unable to hire the few Iraqis with expertise and experience in air traffic control because of De-Ba'athification. Other agencies and bureaucracies across the country were similarly stripped of experts and institutional knowledge. The De-Ba'athification policy continued until 2008 when a more efficient vetting process was implemented. This action by the US polarized the country and contributed to instability and the rise of the Sunni insurgency.[19]

Iraq quickly fell into a civil war as the US military was unable to secure the country or resolve political and cultural problems. As the insurgency grew, foreign nationals who worked for and with the US became immediate targets.

Congressional response. In 2006, the US Congress acknowledged this crisis and created a new Special Immigrant Visa. Congress included Iraqi translators, and other workers in later legislation, in order to evacuate and resettle those targeted because of their relationship with the US or coalition forces. The legislation first approved a limited number of translators. In 2008, the eligibility criteria were expanded and number of visa issues raised.[20] Unlike the experience of Afghans, there appears to have been little foot-dragging on processing SIV applications. In the end, tens of thousands of Iraqi

---

[19] Ibid
[20] Ibid

allies were resettled in the US through the SIV program.

Also unique to Iraq, the US instituted the United States Refugee
Admission Program (USRAP) for Iraqis. USRAP is similar to the SIV
program but does have different eligibility criteria. To be eligible for
the USRAP, a person must be generally displaced from their country of
origin and unable or unwilling to return. An Iraqi who is affiliated with
the US government can apply for either the USRAP or the SIV.[21]

As security in Iraq crumbled, Iraqis displaced as refugees in
Turkey, Syria, and Jordan had exceeded 1.3 million by 2009. USRAP
provided relief for countries that bordered Iraq, where vulnerable
governments were strained by the influx of Iraqi refugees. The US
government's acknowledgement of the precarious situation faced by
these governments provided immediate relief through USRAP.[22] The
US has accepted thousands of Iraqis under this program but has not
extended eligibility to Afghans.[23]

---

[21] US Customs and Immigration Service. (2015, April 24). *Iraqi refugee
processing fact sheet.* Retrieved from
http://www.uscis.gov/humanitarian/refugees-asylum/refugees/iraqi-refugee-
processing-fact-sheet

[22] Cohen, R. (2008). Iraq's displaced: Where to turn? *American University
International Law Review*, 24(2), 301-340. Retrieved from
https://www.brookings.edu/wp-content/uploads/2016/06/10_iraq_cohen.pdf

[23] US Department of State. (2013, May). *U.S. Refugee Admissions Program
(USRAP) Frequently Asked Questions - Iraqi processing.* Retrieved from Bureau
of Population, Refugees, and Migration: https://2009-
2017.state.gov/j/prm/releases/factsheets/2013/210134.htm

The Evacuation

Similar to the SIV process in Afghanistan, Iraqis were not required to process in Guam or any other third country. The Iraqi resettlement process, for a majority of applicants, occurred in Iraq. Applicants applied for and were adjudicated at the embassy in Baghdad. Following successful adjudication, SIV holders boarded planes and flew directly to the US where they resettled either with friends and family or with a resettlement agency.

Since 2007, the USG has provided over $1.7 billion for assistance to Iraqi refugees. The USRAP program alone has resettled hundreds of thousands of Iraqis, far more than the SIV program. From 2006 to 2014, the US admitted over 103,000 Iraqi refugees for resettlement through USRAP.[24] This dwarfs the number of Iraqi SIV issuances as seen in Table 3.3.

---

[24] US Department of State. (2014, May 23). *Iraqi Refugee Resettlement.* Retrieved from Bureau of Population, Refugees, and Migration: https://2009-2017.state.gov/j/prm/releases/factsheets/2014/228685.htm

Table 3.3: SIV for Iraqi translators, interpreters, and employees of the US

Fiscal Year	Principals	Dependents	Total
2007	431	383	814
2008	518	449	967
2009	1,444	1,381	2,825
2010	941	1089	2,030
2011	322	380	702
2012	1,661	2,229	3,890
2013	1,341	2,225	3,566
2014	435	1,079	1,514
2015	334	842	1,176
2016	655	1,595	2,250
2017	553	1,567	2,120
Total	**8,635**	**13,219**	**21,853**

Source: Bureau of Consular Affairs, US Department of State

According to interviews with Iraqi SIV holders in the US, the actual application and processing was fairly simple. The SIV holders interviewed stated that the forms, interview, and issuance was seamless. This could be due to the fact that the embassy in Iraq is the largest embassy in the world and is well staffed with State Department personnel who are responsible for processing the application. The sheer number of SIV and USRAP arrivals indicates that the embassy staff were both prepared and authorized to efficiently process Iraqi SIV applications.

The Arrival and The Resettlement in the US

To date, post-2006 Iraqi resettlement was similar to the South Vietnamese experience in two respects. First, they were similar in size. By the end of fiscal year 2017, the population of Iraqi refugees had increased to just over 160,000. Only 11% of these are SIV holders (see Table 3.4). Second, both SIV and Iraqi refugees are resettling in places other co-ethnics already live. There are some differences between USRAP and SIV settlement patterns. Iraqi refugees are resettling primarily in just five states: California, Michigan, Texas, Arizona, and Illinois. There are also large concentrations in Virginia, Washington, and Massachusetts. Iraqi SIV holders are primarily settling in California, Texas, and Virginia in terms of absolute numbers. As seen with the South Vietnamese and Iraqi Kurd resettlement, post-2006 Iraqis are resettling in places with an existing network of Iraqis to support their integration.

Table 3.4: Iraqi refugee and Special Immigrant Visa resettlement by state through FY2017

	Refugee	SIV		Refugee	SIV		Refugee	SIV
Alabama	478	46	Louisiana	509	69	Oklahoma	283	87
Alaska	49	16	Maine	1,056	123	Oregon	1,634	197
Arizona	8,285	729	Maryland	1,681	353	Pennsylvania	2,909	372
Arkansas	53	15	Massachusetts	4,747	316	Rhode Island	239	41
California	28,495	2,072	Michigan	20,880	765	South Carolina	270	68
Colorado	2,269	634	Minnesota	1,146	149	South Dakota	299	22
Connecticut	1,064	149	Mississippi	14	13	Tennessee	3,108	733
Delaware	8	0	Missouri	2,075	360	Texas	14,317	4,440
District of Columbia	124	20	Montana	20	2	Utah	1,904	207
Florida	2,854	588	Nebraska	1,408	402	Vermont	218	16
Georgia	2,643	238	Nevada	729	60	Virginia	4,604	880
Hawaii	4	0	New Hampshire	547	28	Washington	4,466	663
Idaho	1,618	93	New Jersey	819	107	West Virginia	71	13
Illinois	7,900	775	New Mexico	522	51	Wisconsin	1,244	144
Indiana	544	110	New York	4,364	436	Not Available	2	0
Iowa	688	67	North Carolina	2,129	472			
Kansas	436	32	North Dakota	931	56	**Subtotal**	**14,2534**	**17,754**
Kentucky	2,666	306	Ohio	3,211	317	**TOTAL**	**160,288**	

Source: Bureau of Population, Refugees, and Migration, US Department of State

When evaluating SIV resettlement relative to a state's population, we see a different picture. SIV placement per population is greater in Nebraska, Texas, Colorado, Tennessee, Arizona, and Nevada (see Figure 3.2). With the exception of Texas, this is largely because these states have smaller populations, making any SIV holder and their family more visible.

Figure 3.2: Iraqi SIV resettlement from FY2007-2017

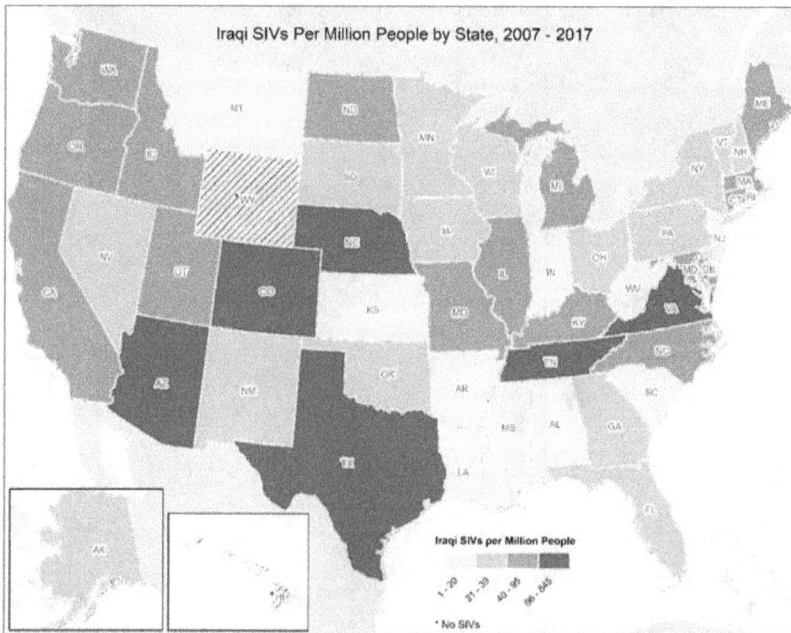

Source: Bureau of Population, Refugees, and Migration. *Admissions & arrivals*. US Department of State. Retrieved from: http://www.wrapsnet.org/admissions-and-arrivals/

The domestic support structure and assistance for Iraqis is the same as other refugees. While the assistance is the same as for Afghans, the resettlement experience was much more varied. According to our interviews, whether an Iraqi SIV holder successfully integrated into the US society depended on multiple factors, including resettlement location, resettlement agency, SIV holder's skills, and family dynamics.

Interviews with non-profit groups that support Iraqi immigrants reported that the support structure for Iraqis is similarly abysmal as it is for Afghans. As seen with Afghan SIV holders, the resettlement agencies placed Iraqi SIV holders in communities that were either outside of the commuting area or in towns that lacked support services for immigrants without a vehicle.

Further, the level of motivation and competency within the resettlement agency was often lacking. One Iraqi interviewee stated that the resettlement agency workers were often other refugees who hardly spoke English and had only been in the US for a short time. His social security paperwork was incorrectly submitted which delayed the receipt of assistance and hampered his ability to integrate in society. Eventually, the living conditions and support was so poor that he moved in with friends who were living nearby. Other interviewees stated that their resettlement agency did a subpar job in helping the SIV holder find a job that is near their home that would earn enough income to feed a family.

According to the GAO, SIV holders have limited options for

government employment in the US.[25] The report's findings were confirmed in an interview with an Iraqi SIV holder who stated that his resettlement town did not have any military base. He was employed by the military, at the highest levels of Special Operations, and was unable to use his language and expertise for employment in the US. After months without a job, he enlisted in the military. He now works remotely with the Defense Language Institute (DLI) as a language instructor for students learning and writing in Arabic.

One SIV holder we interviewed stated that soldiers in the US military who had returned from deployment became an important support network for him and others. Groups of Iraqis and US vets would get together in groups and discuss their situation, what assistance was helping, and gaps in their resettlement experience, especially related to job placement. He said that the Iraqis who worked together on the Special Operations team would fly to Utah for a reunion, which served as a springboard for his eventual employment.

It is worth noting that the Iraqi SIV holders who we interviewed were unmarried and without a family to care for when they arrived in the US. They stated that not having a wife and children made the difficult flight and resettlement much easier. Their ability to travel,

---

[25] Government Accountability Office. (2010). *Iraqi refugees and Special Immigrant Visa holders face challenges resettling in the United States and obtaining US government employment*. Retrieved from http://www.gao.gov/new.items/d10274.pdf

adapt, be unemployed, and mobile would have been very difficult with a family.

In summary

The story of Iraqi evacuation and resettlement begins in 2003 with the US policy of De-Ba'athification which is when the US took ownership of the Iraq's government and aging infrastructure. As part of the rebuilding process, the US employed and relied upon a large number of Iraqis to serve directly for the US government. Numerous political missteps, centrally De-Ba'athification, led to instability across the country.

When civil war broke out, most of these Iraqi employees who worked on behalf of the US became targeted. When legislation was finally passed in 2006 to protect Iraqi allies by allowing them to migrate to the US, the embassy in Baghdad was well prepared and willing to process those SIV and USRAP applications. But, as seen in previous experiences, the resettlement system in the US was not prepared for such a large influx of immigrants. Similar to the Vietnamese evacuation and resettlement, many immigrants who were crucial to the US mission were packed into the US in a short amount of time with little domestic planning.

Concluding Thoughts

The policy mechanism by which allies were (and continue to be) evacuated is different in each of these instances. The resettlement experience also varies considerably. However, what is clear from our interviews is that for the current Afghan and Iraqi SIV holders, the domestic resettlement process is absurdly inadequate. The lack of a consistent policy from evacuation to resettlement is part of the problem. The policy goal of refugees achieving self-sufficiency is simply unattainable under current resettlement policies. The US can and must do better by our allies in order to help them integrate into the US with dignity.

Left to right: SGT Blessing, CPT Bell, CPT Carson

The 209th ANA Kandak formation at Camp Khilighi, Baghlan Province.

CPT Carson attends a meeting at the Baghlan Hospital.

CPT Bell supervises a humanitarian operation in Baghlan-i-Jadid.

CPT Bell observes the 209TH Kandak prepare for a patrol.

CPT Bell and Major Carson pose for a young boy at the Baghlan women's center.

Leadership of the 209th Kandak gather with local leaders.

The 209th Kandak Battalion dedicated a generator to the Baghlan agriculture university.

The 209th Kandak, CPT Carson and Hungarian military attend a ceremony and dedication in Baghlan Providence.

Left to right. Hungarian soldier, CPT Carson, CPT Bell, ANA soldier

PART II

ANALYSIS & FINAL ASSESSMENT

The four diverse ethnic, religious, and cultural groups highlighted in this book arrived in the US with some similarities and many differences that influenced their resettlement experience. To fully understand these successes and challenges, we analyzed each case by evaluating the US context during each resettlement process. Unlike most asylum seekers or other refugees, SIV holders had worked for the US government prior to arriving and were usually somewhat familiar with US customs and culture. However, the political, economic, and socio-cultural contexts in the US varied for each group. This significantly shaped the success and challenges in their resettlement and integration.

Chapter 4 describes our analysis of the role that political, economic, and socio-cultural context played in each resettlement experience. In Chapter 5 we describe the policies and structures that are working well and that should be maintained as well as those that need to be improved, modified, or terminated because they are not contributing to the INA's goal of self-sufficiency.

Chapter 4

Evaluation of Resettlement Policies and Processes

The four diverse ethnic, religious, and cultural groups highlighted in this book arrived in the US with some similarities and many differences that influenced their resettlement experience. To fully understand these successes and challenges, we analyzed each case by evaluating the US context during each resettlement process. Unlike most asylum seekers or other refugees, SIV holders had worked for the US government prior to arriving and were usually somewhat familiar with US customs and culture. However, the political, economic, and socio-cultural contexts in the US varied for each group. This significantly shaped the success and challenges in their resettlement and integration.

❖ ❖ ❖ ❖ ❖

Vietnam

On a large scale and for the first time after a foreign policy failure, the US would mobilize civilian and military personnel to Andersen Air Force Base in Guam, for the reception of foreign nationals fleeing South Vietnam.[1] While the US had received refugees in the past, this

---

[1] This analysis focuses primarily on the second wave of arrivals from Vietnam. See Chapter 2 for more details on the history of admission and resettlement of Vietnamese allies.

was different. The war in South Vietnam came at a cost of life and treasure. Further, this would be the first major defeat of the US in the Cold War and it happened in an embarrassing fashion. However, the South Vietnamese refugees would benefit socially and politically from early support. They were able to overcome challenging economic conditions by creating a niche labor market. Familiarity with US culture and ability to speak English also eased their transition culturally.

Political

The influx of Vietnamese entering the US in 1975 was met with some degree of political and social acceptance that would be unrecognizable in the early 21st century United States. This was the result of political leadership, the menace of the Cold War, an existing community of second-generation Vietnamese immigrants, and less labor market competition from existing immigrant groups.

The welcome started with the Commander in Chief. President Gerald Ford asserted that it was the US' moral obligation to aid and assist the South Vietnamese who were forsaking their country and communism to live in liberty and democracy. He argued that it was our moral and ethical responsibility to resettle and support those who had fought beside us.

In contrast to the early 21st century, a narrow majority of the US public appreciated the argument Ford made. In a poll taken in May of 1975, only 49% opposed the resettlement of South Vietnamese refugees in the US. Although that number may appear high, previous resettlements of Hungarians, Cubans, and Indochinese saw much higher opposition.[2]

The last large scale migration into the US had taken place between 1880 and 1930 with immigrants mostly from southern and eastern Europe.[3] A sizable portion of the working class in the 1970s were second or third generation immigrants, working in unionized jobs. They were not especially hostile to immigration. With caution and skepticism, both the general public and elected officials rallied around Ford's narrative.

The politics of the South Vietnamese resettlement were remarkably non-partisan. Policymakers were less divided and overall supportive of the South Vietnamese resettlement in 1975.[4] Immigration, especially

[2] DeSilver, D. (2015, November 19). *U.S. public seldom has welcomed refugees into country*. Pew Research Center. Retrieved from: http://www.pewresearch.org/fact-tank/2015/11/19/u-s-public-seldom-has-welcomed-refugees-into-country/

[3] Martin, P. (2014, May 19). *Trends in migration to the U.S.* Population Reference Bureau. Retrieved from: http://www.prb.org/Publications/Articles/2014/us-migration-trends.aspx

[4] Elliott, D. (2007, Jan 14). *A lesson in history: Resettling refugees of Vietnam*. Retrieved from National Public Radio: https://www.npr.org/templates/story/story.php?storyId=6855407

from Asia, was never popular in the US. But this effort had supporters among both conservatives and liberals. Opposition by conservatives and especially Republicans, who had worked to limit immigration in the past, may also have been muted because this occurred during the presidency of Republican Gerald Ford.[5]

In addition, policymakers realized that the US had suffered a costly and painful foreign policy defeat. A rejection of South Vietnamese refugees would only deepen the loss of reputation and power. In the mid-1970s, and against the backdrop of the Cold War, denying the resettlement of South Vietnamese would have been viewed globally as an abandonment of the US' allies and a victory for communism.

Economic

One concern for policy makers and the South Vietnamese was the impact that a large influx of workers would have on the economy.[6] The US economy in the 1970s and 1980s suffered from high unemployment, competition for limited social services, and competition in the low-wage job sector among minorities.[7]

---

[5] Scanlan & Loescher, *Calculated Kindness*
[6] Elliott, *A lesson in history: Resettling refugees of Vietnam*
[7] Scanlan & Loescher, *Calculated Kindness*

Unemployment in April of 1974 was 5.1% and spiked to 9.0% in May of 1975 just as Saigon fell.[8]

Two factors contributed to the ability of South Vietnamese refugees successfully overcoming these economic conditions. First, South Vietnamese immigrants thrived in the small service industry by either working in or starting small businesses.[9] Second, inner city housing was much more affordable during this time than it has been for more recent refugees. The combination of a shortage of low wage jobs, a willing workforce, and affordable housing in many cities provided favorable conditions for Vietnamese immigrants to resettle in the US and integrate into society.

It is not that South Vietnamese immigrants were only fit for low wage jobs. Rather, a majority who arrived in the US after the fall of Saigon could only find such work. Since the second wave of refugees were highly educated, spoke English, and had worked with the US government in the past, Vietnamese immigrants were able to fit into the existing labor structure. They entered the job market earning low wages even when their skill set overqualified them for the position. From the 130,000 immigrants who arrived immediately after the fall of

---

[8] Bureau of Labor Statistics. (n.d.). *Labor Force Statistics from the Current Population Survey.* Retrieved from US Department of Labor: https://data.bls.gov/pdq/SurveyOutputServlet

[9] Zhou, M., & Bankston, C. L. (1995). Entrepreneurship. In S. Gall, & I. Natividad (Eds.), *The Asian American almanac: A reference work on Asians in the US* (pp. 511-528). Detriot, MI: Gale Research Inc.

Saigon, the Indochinese employment rate was 94.4% within two years compared to 93.1% for the US.[10]

During the many years of Vietnamese resettlement, the US had a strong middle class. However, the Indochinese did not threaten the jobs of White Americans. Unionized middle-income jobs with benefits represented almost a quarter of the economy. In addition, the relatively low participation rate of women in the workforce left room for these immigrants in the market. In 1975, the rate of women in the workforce was 46.3%. White women specifically had a labor force participation rate of 45.9%. The labor force participation of women with a child in 1975 was 43%.[11] The Vietnamese did not compete in the unionized labor sector nor in the jobs primarily occupied by women. Instead, they created a niche in small industries: fisheries, restaurants, dry cleaning, and small businesses in major cities.

Housing affordability also contributed to the more successful integration of Vietnamese refugees in this time. Urban housing in the mid-1970s was far different than in 2018. The desegregation of schools resulting from the *Brown v. Board* decision[12] and prohibition of racial discrimination in housing under the Fair Housing Act of 1968

---

[10] Scanlan & Loescher, *Calculated Kindness*
[11] US Department of Labor. (n.d.). *Women in the Labor Force*. Retrieved from https://www.dol.gov/wb/stats/NEWSTATS/facts/women_lf.htm#two. The data for women with children was not disaggregated by race.
[12] *Brown v. Board of Education of Topeka*, 347 US 483 (1954)

accelerated "white flight" from all cities across the US. As many Whites moved to the suburbs, they left behind what became affordable housing in many inner cities.[13] In addition, the urban environment was ideal for many immigrants. It allowed them to more easily access medical services, walk to grocery stores, and get around using public transportation. The resettlement agencies and US government initially attempted to resettle the 1975 wave across the US. However, it did not take long for a majority of the population of South Vietnamese to concentrate in inner cities, especially in California and Texas.[14]

Socio-Cultural

The newly arrived immigrants were unsure of their final destination for resettlement in the US, were struggling with mental health challenges following years of war, and were often consigned to jobs well below their skillset. Given those challenges, historians have labeled this resettlement a textbook story of successful assimilation into the United States. Beyond their ethic of hard work and positive attitude, the arrivals had a number of cultural characteristics that eased their integration into the US and acceptance by White Americans.

---

[13] The Data Center. (n.d.). *White Flight*. Retrieved from http://www.datacenterresearch.org/pre-katrina/tertiary/white.html
[14] Wieder, R. (1995). Vietnamese American. In S. Gall, & I. Natividad (Eds.), *The Asian American almanac: A reference work on Asians in the US* (pp. 165-174). Detroit, MI: Gale Research Inc.

Because these refugees worked for the US government, a majority spoke English, were generally better educated, and were accustomed to US culture.[15] In many ways, the US had colonized South Vietnam. In banking, education, and in military and government agencies, South Vietnam had operated as a proxy state of the US since the early 1950s. Hundreds of thousands of US soldiers and civilians had rotated through bases across the country for over two decades. As a consequence, those evacuated and being resettled in the US were familiar with the US culture and lifestyle.

It helped that the majority of Vietnamese practiced Christianity. While most Vietnamese practiced Buddhism, the arrivals were predominantly Catholic, a legacy of almost a century of French colonialism. Catholic churches and parishioners were able to provide a social network, additional aid, and further assist the arrivals' integration into communities across the US. And because Northern Viet Minh were viewed as having an "anti-religious orientation," the resettlement of Southern Vietnamese was framed as refugees fleeing religious persecution.[16]

---

[15] Religious Diversity in Minnesota Initiative. (n.d.). *The Development of Vietnamese Communities in the US*. Retrieved November 22, 2017, from http://religionsmn.carleton.edu/exhibits/show/phat-an-temple/the-development-of-vietnamese-
[16] Ibid

The cultural integration of the South Vietnamese was remarkable. The second wave of Vietnamese arrivals included people who were educated, accustomed to US culture, religiously aligned with Christianity, and proficient in English. This is not to say that Vietnamese refugees did not face discrimination after arriving in the US. The political and social conservative shift in the 1980s certainly affected South Vietnamese refugees. However, as a group, these refugees fared better than many earlier or later immigrants economically and socially. The early social and political support, ability to cope with challenging labor market conditions, and ability to acculturate greatly contributed to the successful resettlement of the South Vietnamese.

❖ ❖ ❖ ❖ ❖

Iraqi Kurds

The Kurdish resettlement mirrored that of the South Vietnamese in the hasty evacuation, route through Guam, and eventual staging in the US prior to resettlement in cities across the US. The major differences between the two resettlements were scale and exposure. While the war in Vietnam lasted decades, the US and coalition forces' presence in Iraq was limited to Operation Provide Comfort between 1991 and 1996. Politically, the Kurdish evacuation was purposefully constructed to remain out of the headlines. This was largely possible because the resettlement numbers were much smaller than those of the South

Vietnamese. Economically, the US was on an upswing that would continue for the next five years. Socially and culturally, the Iraqi Kurds benefited from a previous wave of Iraqi refugees. The Kurdish resettled and integrated into the US culture with much success.

Political

The Kurdish Iraqis were beneficiaries of timing and politics. The Clinton administration was focused on the 1992 re-election against retired Senator and former Majority Leader Bob Dole. The issues of Iraq, Saddam Hussein's actions in the north, and the potential resettlement of Kurds were in plain view of both campaigns. Neither campaign was opposed to, or even particularly interested in, the resettlement of the Iraqi Kurds. Foreign policy decisions and domestic resettlement was not where either party chose to focus.

As late as September of 1996, President Clinton was faced with Saddam Hussein's aggressive moves in northern Iraq and the decision to either resettle immigrants or mobilize military forces back into Iraq. The Dole campaign refrained from politicizing the issue. As the Republican candidate for president, Senator Dole, stated reasonably, "Iraq is a complicated situation."[17]

---

[17] Graham, B., & Balz, D. (1996, Sep 01). Iraqi attack raises U.S. 'concern'. *The Washington Post*. Retrieved from http://www.washingtonpost.com/wp-srv/inatl/longterm/iraq/timeline/090196.htm

In the end, the public was largely unaware of the Kurdish resettlement, which worked to favor the Kurds who did not face large-scale discrimination or bias upon arrival. The foreign policy choice by the Clinton administration to keep forces out of Iraq and remove Kurdish allies was a safe and neutral decision. As was the case with the Vietnamese resettlement, the Kurds had a brief layover in Guam. Here federal, state, and non-profit resettlement agencies were able to work together internally and provide direction for the incoming immigrants. Operation Pacific Haven expedited the evacuation and the processing of the Kurdish refugees. The Department of Defense believed that it would "[u]ndoubtedly be a role model for future humanitarian efforts."[18]

Economic

In the early1990s, the economy began to pick up momentum in major industries. By 1996, favorable conditions prevailed in most major economic indices. The economy of the mid-1990s was strong. Federal and state officials were very concerned with unemployment or saturation of the labor market largely because of the low number of arrivals, which was capped at 6,600.

At the macro level, the labor market rates, unemployment rates, interest rates, and stock market were all trending in a positive direction

---

[18] Cohen, *Iraq's displaced: Where to turn?*

in 1996. The Bureau of Labor Statistics reported 5.1% unemployment in August of 1996, which had been trending down from a high of 7.3% in 1992.[19] The 30-year fixed mortgage rate in August of 1996 was 8.2%, continuing its decline from a high of 11.3% in 1987.[20] The Dow Jones had nearly doubled in a span of six years, from 4,899 in 1990 to 8,806 in 1996.[21] And finally, the consumer sentiment index was 95.3% in August of 1996 compared to 63.9% in October of 1990.[22] Favorable market conditions can create an atmosphere conducive to immigration, and the economy in 1996 was very good, especially when compared the mid-1970s.

US forces typically hire the most educated. According to our interviewees, when the US pulled out and provided visas to the Kurds, a brain drain occurred. Some of the area's smartest minds, politicians, doctors, security officers, and dentists who were vital to their homeland took advantage of the opportunity to leave. While the Kurdish Iraqis came to the US with a variety of skills, they were

[19] Bureau of Labor Statistics. (n.d.). *Databases, tables & calculators by subject: Unemployment*. Retrieved December 6, 2017, from https://www.bls.gov/data/#unemployment
[20] HSH Associates. (n.d.). *HSH's national monthly mortgage statistics: 1986 to 2016*. Retrieved December 6, 2017, from https://www.hsh.com/monthly-mortgage-rates.html
[21] MacroTrends. (n.d.). *Dow Jones - 100 Year Historical Chart*. Retrieved December 6, 2017, from http://www.macrotrends.net/1319/dow-jones-100-year-historical-chart
[22] University of Michigan. (n.d.). *Consumer Sentiment*. St. Louis Federal Reserve Bank. Retrieved from: https://fred.stlouisfed.org/series/UMCSENT

willing to enter the job market at any level. Kurdish Iraqis were not viewed as competing in a tight labor market. Particularly in Nashville, where the largest concentration of Kurdish refugees live, they have served both the domestic and immigrant community well.[23]

Socio-cultural

There have been three small waves of Kurdish immigration to the US, each group established a foundation and path for those following. By the time the second wave arrived in 1996, the Kurdish community had established a network and community for adjustment while maintaining cultural integrity. Kurdish refugees were largely resettled in Nashville, which allowed the existing community to provide the needed support to facilitate adjustment.[24]

More importantly and similar to the South Vietnamese, this wave of Iraqi Kurds spoke English. Through their work with US forces, they became familiar with Western culture. Prior to arrival in the US, Kurds understood Western values, attitudes, and to some degree, the lifestyle.

---

[23] Sawyer, A. M. (2017, June 22). Who are the Kurds, and why are they in Nashville? *The Tennessean.* Retrieved from: http://www.tennessean.com/story/news/local/2017/06/23/who-kurds-and-why-they-nashville/97706968/
[24] Ibid

Further aiding the resettlement in the US, Kurds have a reputation and appreciation for the separation of church and state.[25] While the majority of Kurds identify as Muslim, there is both a more moderate practice of Islam as well as an appreciation for secularism in public life. While the current population of Kurdish Christians in Kurdistan is small, there is also a long history with Christianity among the Kurds.

The Iraqi Kurds were a successful immigration story. This success can be attributed to arriving in small numbers, without political objection, and under favorable economic conditions. Those arriving were amongst the most educated of their people. The economic and socio-cultural conditions were ideal for the INA policy of self-sufficiency. Had the resettlement numbers been larger, had they been dispersed throughout the US, or had they been settled under different economic conditions, the story might have been different.

❖ ❖ ❖ ❖ ❖

Iraq and Afghanistan

In almost every way, the political, economic, and socio-cultural context in the resettlement of Iraqis and Afghans was the opposite of the South Vietnamese and Iraqi Kurds. Despite an extremely polarized

---

[25] Sheppard, S. (2016, October 25). What the Syrian Kurds have wrought. *The Atlantic*. Retrieved from https://www.theatlantic.com/international/archive/2016/10/kurds-rojava-syria-isis-iraq-assad/505037/

Congress, support for the Special Immigrant Visa (SIV) was bipartisan. However, the 2016 election of President Donald Trump and even greater political polarization in Congress has threatened that bipartisanship. The global financial markets crashed in 2007 and the US economy was in turmoil. Socially, overt bias against Muslims in the early 21st century US is widespread. All of these factors have made resettlement difficult for Iraqis and Afghans.

Political

Remarkably, there was political will to authorize the SIV programs before the crisis in Afghanistan and Iraq imploded. Albeit at the last moment and with some reservation, Congress passed legislation authorizing the SIV program relatively early in the wars and continually reauthorized and strengthened the program. With each reauthorization, the number of visas available was increased. All of this was done with bipartisan support. In the 21st century US Congress, rarely has legislation achieved such bipartisan support and continued authorization. The program's support is most notable among veterans. According to Scott Cooper, director of national security outreach at Human Rights First, opposition to the SIV program would generate outrage as "[Congress] would have every veteran's organization in the world calling them out on this."[26]

Legislators on both sides of the aisle have championed the SIV program and did so from 2007 into 2017. Among the many advocates for the SIV in the Senate were John McCain (R-AZ), Jeanne Shaheen (D-N.H.), Jack Reed (D-RI), and Thom Tillis (R-NC). Senator McCain stated in March of 2017,

> *We simply cannot win this war without the assistance of*
> *the Afghan people who put their lives on the line to help*
> *American troops and diplomats serving in harm's way.*
> *Unfortunately in recent years, Congress has reneged on*
> *the promise we made to protect these brave individuals*
> *by failing to authorize the appropriate number of*
> *Special Immigrant Visas for Afghan translators and*
> *interpreters. It's because of our failure that the lives of*
> *thousands of Afghans are in imminent danger from the*
> *Taliban.*[27]

---

[26] Blanchard, E. (2017, Feb 02). Afghan translators hope U.S. visas will arrive before the Taliban does. *Huffington Post*. Retrieved from https://www.huffingtonpost.com/entry/afghan-translators-us-visas-taliban_us_587fbcdae4b0c147f0bca672
[27] *McCain, Shaheen, Reed & Tillis introduce bipartisan bill to authorize 2,500 additional visas for Afghan interpreters.* (2017, March 02). Retrieved from Senator John McCain:
https://www.mccain.senate.gov/public/index.cfm/2017/3/mccain-shaheen-reed-

In the House of Representatives, Representatives Adam Kinzinger (R-Ill.), and Seth Moulton (D-MA), both former military service members, have been outspoken advocates of the SIV. Seth Molton stated,

> *The very least we can do is offer them a chance to stay*
> *alive, to keep living, rather than abandoning them to the*
> *same enemies they united with us to destroy.*[28]

Prominent national security voices in the Department of Defense and US Department of State have also been vocal advocates for the program. National security experts, including General John Nicholson, General Stanley McChrystal, General David Petraeus, and Ambassador Ryan Crocker lobbied Congress through 2016 to support the SIV program, arguing that the credibility of the US is at stake.[29]

At the executive level, support for the SIV program varied across presidencies. There was high levels of support for the SIV programs

tillis-introduce-bipartisan-bill-to-authorize-2-500-additional-visas-for-afghan-interpreters

[28] Lonsdorf, K., & Martin, P. (2016, July 06). Thousands of Afghan interpreters wait for visas as Congress squabbles. *U.S. News & World Report*. Retrieved from https://www.usnews.com/news/articles/2016-07-07/thousands-of-afghan-interpreters-wait-for-visas-as-congress-squabbles

[29] Moulton, S. (2016, Aug 02). *Moulton and bipartisan group of lawmakers to NDAA conferees: Support the Afghan Special Immigrant Visa program.* Congressman Seth Moulton. Retrieved from: https://moulton.house.gov/legislative-center/moulton-and-bipartisan-group-of-lawmakers-to-ndaa-conferees-support-the-afghan-special-immigrant-visa-program/

under the Bush and Obama administrations. President George Bush endorsed the idea when the initial legislation was proposed in 2006. President Barack Obama also signed every reauthorization. However, very early in his presidency, President Trump issued an executive order reducing the number of refugees that the US will accept. President Trump's first executive order on immigration included banning Iraq and Afghan SIV holders. After intense criticism, the executive order was amended to continue the resettlement of SIV recipients.[30]

This shift in support for refugees seen in the Trump administration was also mirrored in Congress. In 2016, former Senator Jeff Sessions (R-AL) and Representative Bob Goodlatte (R-Va.) voiced concern about the potential abuse in the broad selection of Afghans and Iraqis.[31] Congress continues to reauthorize and increase the Afghan

---

[30] Zucchino, D. (2017, Feb 02). Visa ban amended to allow Iraqi interpreters into U.S. *New York Times*. Retrieved from https://www.nytimes.com/2017/02/02/world/middleeast/trump-visa-ban-iraq-interpreters.html

[31] Hauslohner, A., & Demirjian, K. (2016, Dec 01). Afghan visa program extended despite pushback from immigration foes. *The Washington Post*. Retrieved from https://www.washingtonpost.com/news/powerpost/wp/2016/12/02/afghan-visa-program-extended-despite-pushback-from-immigration-foes/?utm_term=.7cf09dd45cb8

SIV program. There has been no authorizations for the Iraqi SIV since the National Defense Authorization Act (NDAA) for FY 2014.[32]

The current SIV programs do have grassroots, sometimes veteran led, social support and public education efforts that was absent in past resettlements. Several non-profit organizations have been established to aid and resettle Iraqi and Afghan veterans of the wars. Among them, No One Left Behind,[33] Iraq Mutual Aid Society,[34] Iraqi Refugee Assistance Project,[35] and the List Project[36] are specifically dedicated to Iraqi and Afghans SIV holders. Beyond the resettlement agencies with a charter and relationship with the Department of State, these organizations were founded and operate independently of the US government's efforts. Their charters include educating policymakers, raising money for the SIV holder, and keeping the US public aware of the challenges in maintaining the program.

---

[32] US Department of State & US Department of Homeland Security. (2018, April 2018). *Joint Department of State/Department of Homeland Security report: Status of the Iraqi special immigrant visa program.* US Department of State. Retrieved from https://travel.state.gov/content/dam/visas/SIVs/Report_of_the_Iraqi_SIV_Program-October_2017.pdf

[33] No One Left Behind. (n.d.). *Home.* Retrieved from http://nooneleft.org/

[34] Iraqi Mutual Aid Society. (n.d.). *Home.* Retrieved from http://www.iraqimutualaid.org

[35] Now called the International Refugee Assistance Project. International Refugee Assistance Project. (n.d.). *Home.* Retrieved from Urban Justice Center: https://refugeerights.org/

[36] The List Project to Resettle Iraqi Allies. (n.d.). *Home.* Retrieved from http://thelistproject.org

The political will in Congress to maintain the program has lasted more than a decade but the future is uncertain. While the wars in Iraq and Afghanistan remain active in 2018, the US American public is ambivalent. Immigration, specifically from Muslim countries, faced restriction from the Trump administration's 2017 executive order. As one of the few bipartisan programs left, it is not clear whether the SIV can withstand the current trend towards nationalism.

Economic

Although the first authorization for the SIV was passed in 2006, Iraqis and Afghans did not begin to arrive until 2007. The arrival of SIVs from Iraq and Afghanistan coincided with the global economic and financial crisis that began in early 2007 and reached a peak of market failure in mid-2008.[37] With the global financial crisis, unemployment soared, bank lending tightened, and underfunded social programs became even more strained.

As the global financial crisis peaked, unemployment in February of 2009 was 9.5%. The unemployment rate for minorities, who comprise the majority of workers in entry-level and low-income positions, was even higher. Unemployment for Black Americans in 2010 was over

---

[37] Guillén, M. F. (2017, Dec 12). *The global economic & financial crisis: A timeline*. Philadelphia, PA: The Lauder Institute, University of Pennsylvania. Retrieved from https://lauder.wharton.upenn.edu/wp-content/uploads/2015/06/Chronology_Economic_Financial_Crisis.pdf

15% and among Hispanics it reached 12%. Job openings during the financial crisis decreased 44%. In February of 2009, the US economy laid off 326,392 workers. From 2007-2009, the employment decline was greater than any recession in recent decades.[38]

Compared to previous resettlement periods, the US economy's ability to absorb large numbers of immigrants had changed drastically. Wages had significantly stagnated, technology and continued economic restructuring had eliminated many middle income jobs, and the market for the low-wage jobs that remained was saturated.[39] Union jobs have also greatly declined. Union membership in 2016 was at 10%, half of what it was in the mid-1970s.[40] Finally, there are far more women in the workforce than ever before. In 2016, the labor participation rate of women with a child was 68%.[41]

Adding to the challenges for refugees, urban living, which was affordable in previous resettlements, has become expensive. The return of White Americans to the city, increased speculation in residential

---

[38] Bureau of Labor Statistics. (2012, Feb). *The recession of 2007–2009.* Retrieved from US Department of Labor: https://www.bls.gov/spotlight/2012/recession/
[39] Rosenfeld, J., Denice, P., & Laird, J. (2013, Aug 30). *Union decline lowers wages of nonunion workers.* Economic Policy Institute. Retrieved from: http://www.epi.org/publication/union-decline-lowers-wages-of-nonunion-workers-the-overlooked-reason-why-wages-are-stuck-and-inequality-is-growing/
[40] Bureau of Labor Statistics. (2018, January 19). *Union Members Summary.* Retrieved from https://www.bls.gov/news.release/union2.nr0.htm
[41] US Department of Labor, *Women in the Labor Force*

housing, and city sanctioned housing development that emphasizes luxury housing and amenities fuel this problem.[42]

As cities became unaffordable, SIV holders have been pushed into suburban or rural communities. Rural and suburban living is cheaper and therefore the government's budget for rental assistance stretches further. However, placing refugees in the suburbs or in rural areas relegates them to places with limited jobs within walking distance. Most SIV holders do not have vehicles upon arrival nor do they have the credit to qualify for a loan to purchase one. This makes achieving the INA goal of self-sufficiency much more difficult to achieve.

In addition, suburban and rural places rarely have medical facilities with culturally or linguistically competent services appropriate for refugees fleeing war torn countries. Placing SIV holders in suburban or rural location may unnecessarily increases the risk for unmonitored or undiagnosed physical or mental health problems among individual SIV holders and their families.

Socio-cultural

While Iraqis and Afghans resettled under the same visa program, during the same timeframe, under similar legislation, and with the

---

[42] Katz, B., & Wagner, J. (2008, June 1). *Transformative investments: Remaking American cities for a new century*. Brookings Institution. Retrieved from: https://www.brookings.edu/articles/transformative-investments-remaking-american-cities-for-a-new-century/

same benefits and resettlement agencies, their experiences in the US presents a stark contrast. While Iraqis have found a base of support and sense of community, Afghans have struggled to effectively resettle in a similar manner.

Iraqis, including Sunni, Shia, and Kurds, have a resettlement history in the US. Communities across the US in Michigan, California, and Illinois have created networks to support new arrivals.[43] Also, Iraq is considered a more modern and Westernized society among Middle Eastern countries. Under Saddam Hussein, strict Islamist teaching was suppressed. Music, arts, math, languages, and medicine taught from a Western perspective were available to some degree in the universities in Baghdad as well as in other major cities. The Iraqi education system at the university level was considered to be diverse in content and perspective.[44]

In contrast, while Afghans have migrated to the US over the years, the numbers have been far smaller. Afghans have settled in communities in the US but not nearly at the scale or with the social

---

[43] Grieco, E. (2003, April 01). *Iraqi immigrants in the United States*. Retrieved from Migration Policy Institute: https://www.migrationpolicy.org/article/iraqi-immigrants-united-states-0

[44] Nixon, J. (2016). *Debriefing the president: The interrogation of Saddam Hussein*. New York, NY: Blue Rider Press.

support system as seen with Iraqis.[45] As a result, the community network that the Vietnamese, Kurds, and Iraqis benefited from has been lacking for the Afghan community.

Compounding this is that Afghan society itself is dominated by tribal divisions. Religiously, Afghans are comprised of Sunni and Shias but socially the culture is far more ethnically diverse. The major Afghan ethnic groups consist of Pashto, Tajik, Hazara, Uzbek, Aimeq, and Turkmen. Collectively, these groups struggle to join and work together in Afghanistan and share little sense of national identity. For the average Afghan, tribe or ethnic group identity often comes before Afghan national identity.[46]

This absence of unity among Afghan SIV holders has been accompanied by lack of a nationwide and effective grassroots support network by or for Afghans. Of the four non-profit organizations described earlier that provide assistance to and educate the public and policymakers about SIV holders, only one provides support for Afghans.

---

[45] US Census Bureau. (n.d.). *American Fact Finder*. Retrieved from https://factfinder.census.gov/faces/tableservices/jsf/pages/productview.xhtml?src=bkmk
[46] Bruno, G. (2008, November 05). *A tribal strategy for Afghanistan*. Retrieved from Council on Foreign Relations: https://www.cfr.org/backgrounder/tribal-strategy-afghanistan

Another dramatic difference between the resettlement of Iraqi and Afghan allies and previous groups is the widespread and entrenched bias against the Muslim community post 9/11. The Vietnamese and Kurds also experienced discrimination. There were even localized incidents of violence against Vietnamese refugees, especially in the 1980s. However, the global war on terror and media preoccupation with terrorist attacks by people claiming to act in the name of Islam has fostered a wider and deeper backlash against Muslims and people perceived to be Muslim. The growth of radical Islam and the fear surrounding terrorism does not aid the ability of SIV holders and their families to adjust and integrate into society. This level of bias and discrimination only adds to the already difficult task of immigrating into any society.

Further, both the Iraq and Afghan SIV holders are resettled throughout the US. Unlike with Iraqi Kurds or Vietnamese refugees, Iraqi and Afghan SIV holders have been distributed across the country, often in places without an existing social network. The resettlement location is determined by the Department of State in coordination with the nine contracted non-profit organizations. For example, the organization may only have a resettlement option open in Youngstown, Ohio. There may be no community of Afghans or Iraqis in Youngstown, leaving the arrivals without a local network to support their transition.

Unless the SIV holder can identify a direct family link and is willing to forfeit resettlement benefits, the SIV holder is assigned to what amounts to a randomly selected state and city at the embassies in Baghdad or Kabul. The resettlement agency is then alerted to the flight arrival. This process places SIV holders throughout the US without even a basic evaluation or consideration of their skills, desires, or family needs. This puts a significant strain on the ability of the SIV holder and family to adjust and integrate.

Conclusion

The prior resettlement process was staged in Guam for Vietnamese and Kurds. This gave refugees the opportunity to decompress and focus on their new life. In the current process, the resettlement agency interacts with the SIV holder and family for the first time at the airport when they arrive in the US. Many of the SIV holders from Iraq and Afghanistan have been living under threat for years, in combat, with families on the run throughout the country. Beyond the understandable culture shock, the resettlement process deviated from the successful practices found in the resettlement of previous allies and did so during a politically, economically, and socio-culturally challenging context. In the current environment, the process for resettling SIV holders makes achieving economic self-sufficiency very difficult.

Chapter 5

Final Assessment

The current refugee resettlement process is an artifact of the 1950s and is not acceptable for current SIV holders. According to the Immigration and Naturalization Act, the primary goal in the resettlement of SIV holders is to "achieve economic self-sufficiency among refugees as quickly as possible."[1] In 1965, the coordination among agencies, the funding allocated, the national and global economy, and the socio-political and cultural context supported this objective. However, while the economy and economic context of the US has changed dramatically, the system for achieving self-sufficiency has not. There are some policies, structures, and funding models that support the goal of self-sufficiency. At the same time, the overall system is out of sync with resettlement needs in the 21st century. This is especially the case with current Iraqi and Afghan SIV holders.

Federal and State Agencies

At the state level, state agencies serve as middle management to fulfill the INA policy goal of self-sufficiency. State agencies oversee non-profit resettlement agencies, serve as liaisons with federal

---

[1] Immigration and Nationality Act of 1965, 8 USC §412(a)(1)(A)(i)

agencies, and have the strategic vision for efficient use of their state's capacity. This structure works well because staff at state agencies know their own support systems and socio-cultural context better than staff at national agencies do. Maintaining relationships between national and state level agencies is crucial to ensuring that SIV holders are settled appropriately.

However, based on our interviews as well as other published reports evaluating the refugee resettlement process, we find that the assistance provided to SIV holders do not fully support, and in some ways undermine, this objective. Even in states with strong medical care systems and robust labor markets, there are significant challenges to effectively supporting SIV holders and their families. State agencies consistently and legitimately question whether self-sustainability can be realistically achieved with the current funding, policies, and economy. Of particular concern is inability to transfer of benefits across states, the lack of consideration for the transportation needs of refugees settled in suburban or rural locations, and the limited attention paid to matching the health needs of refugees with available medical care.

What's working

There is no uniform federal policy on the management of state resettlement agencies. Because of this, each state operates and funds resettlement services differently. In 38 states, a state refugee coordinator and state refugee resettlement agency is funded from the state budget. In 12 states, the refugee coordinator is delegated to one of the nine volunteer agencies (known as Volags) appointed by the Office of Refugee Resettlement (ORR) and overseen by the federal Department of Health and Human Services (HHS).[2] We find that funding the resettlement agency from the state budget is a model that works very well to ensure that the resettlement process is attentive to both the needs of the refugee and to local conditions.

From our interviews, we found that state funded refugee agencies are more invested in the success of the SIV holder in their respective state and their integration into local society. Compared to states where Volags run resettlement services, the state refugee coordinator become subject matter experts who provides knowledge, expertise, and strategic oversight of the Volags.

This particular structure also appears to make the executive and legislative branches more invested in the success of refugee resettlement. We found that where Volags run the state resettlement services, refugees are simply one more external interest group to balance against the rest. In short, without internal commitment that comes with funding a publicly operated agency dedicated to resettlement, SIV holders and other refugees become less important

---

[2] See Appendix B for a fuller description of the organizational structure and the role of Volags in particular.

and consequently subject to shifting legislative priorities and budget constraints.

What's not working

According to interviews with state agencies, SIV holders are given a limited financial and medical assistance package under the assumption that this incentivizes self-sufficiency rather than dependency on the government. However, state agencies consistently stated that the assistance package is insufficient and does not support mobility within the state nor interstate travel for employment. Further, the medical assistance provided is not uniform throughout the US and often lacks preventative and mental health care. In addition, the complexity of the US medical care system makes SIV holders and other refugees vulnerable to falling through the cracks. The combination of lack of consistency in available support across states and the effectively random placement for resettlement makes successful adjustment, integration, and achievement of self-sufficiency very difficult.

The inattention to transportation needs of SIV holders and their families in particular works against the US policy for self-sufficiency. A transportation deficit severely inhibits the SIV holder's ability to attend medical and social service appointments, job training or job interviews, or language instruction. Because refugee assistance does not include driver's training or subsidies to purchase a vehicle, SIV holders are limited to public transportation. The reliance on public transit is especially problematic where SIV holders are settled in car-dependent places. Resettlement agencies argued that the cost of living is cheaper in rural areas compared to urban areas that have regular rail and bus service. However, the hours of operation and routes in suburban or rural public transit systems, where they exist, often does not coincide with shift work or employment outside of the commuting area. Further, having to use public transportation for a family with small children could discourage SIV holders from attending crucial medical and other resettlement appointments that would lead to self-sufficiency.

Current administrative policy and procedures make transferring assistance across state lines impossible. If a SIV holder was resettled in Maryland and shortly upon arrival was offered a position in South Dakota, the resettlement agency in Maryland would not be able to assist because it lacks an administrative channel to transfer costs, payments, or even the file to South Dakota. Since the SIV holder was not originally resettled in South Dakota, the resettlement agencies in South Dakota would not receive payments from the federal government for services rendered. These same barriers exist for transferring medical insurance support.

The funding for the eight months of medical insurance is provided to the state. States bill the federal government for the entire eight months of the medical insurance in one invoice. If the SIV holder leaves the state, under the current system, the state cannot transfer the unused insurance to another state since medical insurance systems vary across states. The receiving state cannot apply for funding for any of the medical insurance provided to the SIV holder. In effect, if a SIV holder moves across state lines, he and his family will lose their medical insurance unless employer-sponsored health insurance is provided.

Other research also suggests that eight months of medical care assistance is simply insufficient. In the post-2008 economy, employer provided medical care insurance is uncommon for the entry level jobs that many SIV holders are able to get. According to the GAO, it often takes 9-12 months for SIV holders to find employment. Even if they do, there is no guarantee that medical insurance will be provided by the employer.[3]

An additional problem related to access to health and medical care is that medical insurance systems are not uniform across states. For example, states that have expanded Medicaid coverage under the Affordable Care Act (ACA) to adults under 65 with income up to 133% of the federal poverty level, such as California, are able to provide medical coverage for most SIV holders and their family beyond the mandatory eight months. Unless the SIV holder gains

---

[3] Government Accountability Office, *Iraqi refugees and Special Immigrant Visa holders face challenges*

insurance through an employer, states that have not accepted the ACA expansion, such as Tennessee, will leave SIV holders uninsured after eight months. SIV holders are clearly better off in some states than others. Our research suggests that access to medical insurance is not taken into consideration during the process of deciding where to settle SIV holders.

The lack of mental health coverage in the medical assistance provided to SIV holders also works against the goal of self-sufficiency. SIV holders and their family come to the US from a war zone where they have been living, sometimes on the run, for many years. Many of these arrivals have serious underlying post-traumatic stress and physical illnesses that are not accounted for in the funding for medical care.[4] Lack of mental health coverage to treat trauma and other emotional health problems will likely hinder obtaining or maintaining employment as well as hamper the adjustment and integration of the SIV holder and his family.

Further, SIV holders and family members are often unfamiliar with Western medical practices and systems. According to Lipson and Meleis, the Western medical system is extremely bureaucratic compared to the Middle East. Cultural and communication barriers are

---

[4] International Rescue Committee. (2009). *Iraqi refugees in the United States: In dire straits.* New York, NY.

widespread.[5] Current SIV holders and their family are a vulnerable population that, because of the random placement for resettlement, often lack a supportive social network and have significant health risks that, if untreated, could cause harm to individuals and society. This can easily be prevented by adding mental health coverage to the initial medical insurance assistance provided to SIV holders.

Many of the problems shared with us by state resettlement agencies as well as found in national evaluations suggest that the random placement of SIV holders and their families is a large part of the problem. SIV holders could be assigned to a state with better or worse assistance packages, often without their knowledge or choice. The random placement and lack of transferability means that the average SIV holder loses medical benefits before acquiring employment.[6] In addition, the variation in available social support across states means that SIV holders without a network or other material resources are at risk of becoming homeless. The "Resettlement Lottery," as the International Rescue Committee terms it, simply does not support the goal of self-sufficiency.[7]

SIV Holders – Mutual support and aid

---

[5] Lipson, J. G., & Meleis, A. I. (1983). Issues in health care of Middle Eastern patients. *Western Journal of Medicine*, 139(6), 854-861.
[6] Government Accountability Office, *Iraqi refugees and Special Immigrant Visa holders face challenges*
[7] International Rescue Committee, *Iraqi refugees in the United States*

SIV holders and their family endure an exhaustive and sometimes cumbersome application process to escape the threat of insurgents who are targeting them because of their relationship with the US. SIV holders have practical experience in working with the US government in a war zone and are extremely motivated. Upon arrival, however, SIV holders are faced with a decentralized resettlement process, a completely new and complicated health care system, and very limited assistance package. The randomly selected state and city he is resettled in has an enormous influence on the success or failure of the SIV holder. Those with access to grassroots organizations established for the sole purpose of supporting current SIV holders are better off and less dependent on the resettlement agencies.

What's working

In our interviews with SIV holders, gratitude was a consistent theme. They deeply appreciate the opportunity to live in the US. The SIV holders we spoke with were honored and excited to live in the US no matter how difficult the application process and resettlement were. One Iraqi interviewee stated:

> *I lost everything while working for the US. I knew that America was bigger than a resettlement agency. At the end, I came to America to carry on with our lives. The overall experience until you get to the United States is, I think, it's looked upon in a positive way. People*

appreciate the help of the government and the
legislations that are in place to help these people that
helped the US government.

We found two conditions that best supported integration and self-sufficiency. One is placement in areas with access to grassroots organizations dedicated to supporting the specific refugee group. The various Mutual Aid Associations supporting the South Vietnamese resettlement are the best historic example of this. Currently, the Iraqi Mutual Aid Society provides similar support in Chicago, Illinois.

The other condition is placement near immigrants from similar cultural groups and languages. The social support from those who speak your language and know your culture has been repeatedly shown to increase the success of resettled allies and their families. In the case of the Kurdish resettlement, a large portion of Iraqi Kurds immigrated to Tennessee in 1991 following the first Iraq War (i.e., the Gulf War). This laid the foundation for a network that aided the resettlement of Iraqi Kurds in 1996. A Kurdish interviewee stated:

Perhaps Americans thought because there is a huge
Kurdish community in Nashville, if we send these
people, the Americans would not have to look after
them. It would be easier for them to live with their
fellow Kurds, and then the Kurds who were in Nashville
before their arrival, they would be helping them, which

I think it was a smart decision, good perception,
because once they arrived in Nashville, people did help
them to find a job, to resettle, to make it better for
themselves.

What's not working

The current system is barely manageable for SIV holders who arrive with no spouses or other dependents. SIV holders who come with a wife or children experience significant challenges because of the poorly structured, underfunded, and overburdened refugee assistance system. SIV holders with a wife or children carry a heavier burden when faced with setbacks or unmet expectations. One interviewee stated:

Because I was a single guy, I had many friends. I had
money. I came speaking English. I was able to do things
on my own. I've seen families that are struggling. They
were left alone. They couldn't do anything about it
because of the resettlement agency.

The settlement location is a critical determinant of success or failure. In all four conflicts, immigrants were given a choice to settle in the US at a specific, desired location or as directed by the resettlement agency. Currently, if immigrants choose to relocate with a close family member, friend, or near existing co-ethnic communities, comprehensive resettlement assistance is not always provided. Those who do not choose a specific place are relocated based on the Volags' vacancies across the US. A report sponsored by the Hollings Center for International Dialogue illustrates how placement affects the ability to obtain employment and how this can be particularly challenging for SIV holders with families.

> *One interviewee living in San Diego described how his friend who had been a guard at the U.S. embassy had called him to ask advice since he had just been granted a visa. The guard was planning on heading to San Diego since he knew some people there, but the interviewee was concerned. The man had 8 children and did not know how to drive. In Afghanistan, one working man could support such a family, but how was he going to do this in America? Especially in San Diego, you needed a car to get anywhere. He didn't want the man to think he was unwilling to help him, but he thought he should perhaps tell him to consider settling elsewhere.[8]*

The SIV holders that we interviewed stated that the resettlement location is a coin toss in their experience. In some cases, they are

---

[8] Coburn & Sharan, *Out of harm's way? Perspectives of the special immigrant visa program for Afghans*, p.10

placed in an area with job opportunities, public transportation, and immigrant-friendly cultures. In other cases, immigrants are left to forge their own path in unfriendly areas lacking jobs and transportation. According to one SIV holder, he was placed in Indianapolis, Indiana. However, he had served and had maintained contact with members of the Massachusetts Army National Guard. After arriving in Indiana and finding few employment prospects and no real social network, he contacted his friends and moved to Massachusetts.

Due to budget constraints, refugees are resettled in affordable neighborhoods, which often already possess a large supply of lower-wage workers. This effectively places SIV holders in places with heavy labor market competition. As a consequence, they have a hard time finding jobs in the local area, forcing them look outside the commuting area for work. Employment opportunities in some cases require transportation that does not exist. The lack of reliable public transportation across the suburban and rural communities in the US where SIV holders are frequently placed forces them to scramble to buy a car. SIV holders come to the US with little or no savings. Purchasing a quality vehicle requires financing, which immigrants are unable to get because they lack a credit history.

Further, resettlement agencies and medical appointments are often not in the same location. Without transportation, interviewees reported having to choose which appointment they are able to get to or to travel in taxis. We also frequently heard about limited availability of health care providers forcing SIV holders and their families to either wait months for an appointment at a local health care facility or travel beyond their commuting capability. Without reliable and accessible public transportation or a vehicle, gaining employment or accessing needed medical and social services becomes extremely challenging.

The government does its best to educate refugees about the assistance they will get before they depart for the US. Resettlement agencies also work hard to help them navigate complicated bureaucracies. Nevertheless, every SIV holder and his family comes to the US with different challenges, goals, and expectations. An immigrant with post-traumatic stress, dependent children who is settled in locations with high labor market competition is in a vastly different position than a healthy refugee who comes to the US alone and settles near family or friends. The refugee resettlement system is simply not designed to support SIV holders or their families who struggle in an unfamiliar environment without transportation or a social support system.

Not all states, resettlement agencies, and towns are equal. The range of success and failure of an immigrant, scaled out, depends on several variables. One immigrant we interviewed stated that the resettlement agency failed to pay the landlord on time, which led to his two-child family's eventual eviction. After spending all their resettlement time and money at a hotel, he was unable to find employment, and his credit history was crushed.

In contrast, better established resettlement agencies in other towns were able to work with landlords as the rent payments were delayed. From a health and social perspective, immigrants experience communities that are accommodating as well as communities that are unable to integrate immigrants or service their particular needs.

Voluntary Agencies

Voluntary agencies, known as Volags, are on the front lines of the refugee resettlement process. They take on the responsibility of assisting immigrants with great pride. The Volags have been in place for decades and are built into the fabric of refugee resettlement. These nine agencies, and dozens of field offices and hundreds of satellite offices, serve as institutional knowledge for past, current, and future resettlement. From the national headquarters to the local offices, these individuals are passionate about their work and overloaded with cases.

What's working

The level of positive communication between Volags and state immigration offices in the states interviewed is remarkable. This works in the best interest of the newly arrived immigrants. In an interview with a state office staffer about the relationship between Volags and state offices:

I think if I had major concerns about a county, 'Hey,
you've proposed 600 refugees in a county that normally
gets 130. I have serious concerns about that; that can't
happen.' I think they would hear that.

In some places, resettlement agencies are now beginning to coordinate more consistently with local leaders in the places where they resettle refugees. This relationship was lacking for many years which created problems that the state immigration office was often too small to address. The local Volags should be meeting with local officials before placing immigrants into their community. Where this coordination is happening, the school district's English language learning capacity, available affordable housing, existing medical services, and potential employment opportunities are discussed. This coordination helps localities identify where and how to fill in the gaps when resettlement services fall short. It also helps the agencies determine whether a particular city or town is better for a particular family.

What's not working

Caseworkers at the ground level have far too many cases to pay proper attention to each file. Since the 2006 SIV legislation, the caseworkers in states that typically accept a large number of immigrants have had two to three times their typical case load. According to a 2010 GAO report, a local Volag office had budgeted and expected to serve 300 refugees in 2009 but received 1,200. In 2008, the average case load was 30 per caseworker and spiked to 120 the following year.[9] Overburdened agencies cannot be expected to provide the level of service an individual SIV holder may need. It also serves as a barrier to developing innovative approaches to effectively serve the unique situation of SIV holders.

We found that resettlement offices either lack the capacity or are reluctant to operate outside their prescribed procedures and historic practices. Most agencies see a diverse group of refugee and immigrants. Others have a steady flow of one particular group. In general, the resettlement agencies do not pool resources or cater to an arriving community. In addition to often having an extremely large caseload, Volags lack the dynamic, creative capability to provide personal attention to the unique needs of SIV holders and their families.

In our interviews with Afghan SIV holders, their gratitude for the opportunity provided by resettlement is also mixed with dismay that they are unable work at their fullest potential. In most cases, the skills and education of SIV holders are not tailored to jobs or regions they are placed nor are they enhanced once they arrive. Many SIV holders are highly educated, have worked in leadership positions with the US

---

[9] Government Accountability Office, *Iraqi refugees and Special Immigrant Visa holders face challenges*

military or diplomatic services, have been project managers on multi-million dollar contracts, or are lawyers, doctors, nurses, accountants, or other trained professional. We heard in our interviews that Volags regularly direct such SIV holders to manual labor type jobs and do not spend the time and effort to transfer their education and skill set to the US. For a foreign born professional, the process of obtaining a nursing, accounting, or medical license is daunting and requires dedicated support beyond the one year time limit written in current law.[10] The research on SIV holders sponsored by the Hollings Center for International Dialogue found similar frustrations.

> *I am so grateful for the SIV program. Afghans have few opportunities to save themselves and it gave me a chance to start a new life in America ... [but] ... It has been very hard trying to figure out how to live here.*[11]

Although coordination with city and county officials is happening at some locations, the practice is not standard and is largely dependent on the personalities and leadership within the individual agency. The common practice of placing a SIV holder in an affordable housing unit without alerting local officials and without knowing the city's infrastructure in not the best interests of the immigrant. Again we find

---

[10] See Appendix A for legal limitations regarding job training and recertification.
[11] Coburn & Sharan, *Out of harm's way? Perspectives of the special immigrant visa program for Afghans*, p. 3

that random resettlement in combination with lack of local coordination creates unnecessary risk for the SIV holder and his family.

Advocacy Groups

Several non-profit organizations have sprung up to advocate specifically for Iraq and Afghan SIV holders. Some of the most prominent groups are the Iraqi Refugee Assistance Project (IRAP),[12] The List Project,[13] and No One Left Behind.[14] These organizations attempt to fill in the gaps in much the same way as the Mutual Assistance Associations (MAAs) did for the South Vietnamese. The more recent groups formed after the stories of mismanagement and organizational inefficiencies in the resettlement of SIV holders were exposed. These groups provide comprehensive services to Iraqi and Afghan arrivals, legal services for immigrants in the US and those still seeking refuge, and political advocacy for additional services and more effective legislation.

What's working

Each group serves a specific function or provides a service that is unique and valuable for incoming immigrants. Generally, the services

---

[12] Now called the International Refugee Assistance Project. See International Refugee Assistance Project, *Home*
[13] (The List Project to Resettle Iraqi Allies, n.d.)
[14] No One Left Behind, *Home*

provided do not overlap. One organization provides legal services for incoming immigrants while another provides money for furniture or the purchase of a car. Another group works with SIV applicants who have not been approved due to bureaucratic delays. From a strategic perspective, this is an efficient use of resources.

The groups have worked together and with Congressional staff to enhance and broaden the current legislation. Together, the organizations serve as advocates and a resources for legislators who are interested in assisting SIV holders. Whereas the resettlement agencies aid and assist SIV holders and other refugees, these non-profit organizations focus specifically on the concerns and welfare of SIV holders and their family. The organization's successful lobbying effort is largely responsible for the extension and expansion of the current Afghan SIV program.

What's not working

The role of these advocacy groups in bridging the gaps in the current refugee resettlement and advocating on their behalf cannot be understated. However, the organizations are small in number and size. The groups largely operate at a national level and do not have local centers in the way the Vietnamese MAAs did. Although we find their effort and work to be amazing, SIV holders would be better off if there were more organizations of this type at the local level.

PART III

RECOMMENDATIONS & CONCLUSION

The US has twice successfully evacuated, admitted, and resettled foreign nationals whose lives were threatened because of their work for and with the US government. Unfortunately, the admission and resettlement of current SIV holders from Afghanistan and Iraq has not evolved to take into account the current political, economic, or socio-cultural context. We make recommendations in Chapter 6 to strengthen the refugee resettlement system with a particular focus on supporting current SIV holders from Iraq and Afghanistan.

We conclude in Chapter 7 with a summary of the precarious future of the SIV program. The SIV program needs stronger Congressional direction, state level leadership, and public support in order to make good on our special obligation to current Afghan and Iraqi allies.

Chapter 6

Recommendations

The current SIV process can be characterized as inconsistent and inefficient. Congress and the president were quick to act in 2006 by creating, and later enhancing, legislation to authorize the SIV. In the 2006 SIV legislation, Congress and the president acted with speed. The legislation had proponents among the public and Department of Defense. However, the creation of legislation alone is not enough. In short, the SIV policy created in 2006 was legislatively efficient but bureaucratically inefficient.

Federal agencies lack the willingness or ability to retain the lessons learned from previous experiences of resettling foreign nationals whose lives were put at risk because of their relationship with the US. The leadership to address the challenges that come with interagency relationships in the implementation of the current SIV program is also lacking. To this day, the SIV process from visa issuance to resettlement does not have a defined leader who answers to Congress or the president. Instead, a group of agencies and civil servants are left to piece together a policy and process until this SIV program is terminated. Policies like the current SIV programs do not have a matter of years for agencies to work out the kinks. As seen in both the

Vietnamese and Kurdish experiences, the window for effective agency action is extremely narrow.

Self-sufficiency is the primary goal of the Immigration and Nationality Act (INA). This singular focus has driven all of the policies, practices, and assistance provided to refugees, including SIV holders. There are valid questions about the legitimacy of the self-sufficiency goal. We too believe that Congress should periodically review the goals of the refugee programs. Our recommendations presume that self-sufficiency will likely remain the primary goal in refugee resettlement for the foreseeable future. We feel that we have a responsibility to improve the system as it is currently structured in the INA while the very important debates around the merits of self-sufficiency as a goal play themselves out.

To achieve self-sufficiency, the US policy is to provide minimal and time-limited social and medical services to incentivize independence. With the arrival of South Vietnamese immigrants following the fall of Saigon in the 1970s, self-sufficiency was achievable in the US economy and social structure. For the Kurdish Iraqis in 1996, favorable conditions existed that allowed for adjustment and integration. By 2006, the economic and social environment in the US had changed. Currently, self-sufficiency is extremely difficult and potentially unachievable without changes to current policies and practices. The four case studies evaluated here provide guidance on closing current gaps and expanding on what has worked historically and today.

Prioritize SIV applications from those working with Special Forces

SIV applications from those who work with Special Operations Forces should be prioritized over those who work in safer locales with less insurgent action. The Iraq and Afghan staff at the embassies do not share a fraction of the risk of those serving with Special Operations Forces, especially those in remote outposts. When embassy staff applications are taken more seriously or processed more quickly than the local hires working where insurgent activities is greatest, it raises questions about abuse of the program. Local hires who are most likely to receive substantive threats to their life, or the lives of their family, are those working in the field with Special Operations Forces. It is here where insurgent activity is greatest and where local hires are at greatest risk.

Evaluating the most-at-risk is challenging but will add legitimacy to the program. Without constraints, the program is susceptible to repeated abuse and becomes vulnerable in Congress. Given the nationalistic trend in the US as well as the hyper-partisan national politics playing out as we write this, the SIV program is vulnerable to significant modification or even cancellation. It would be too easy to point to perceived abuses in the SIV program to justify such drastic actions. Developing systems to prioritize or fast track those at higher risk, as well as reducing abuse of the process by those with personal relationships in the embassy, will improve the legitimacy of the program and ensure its longevity for the duration of US involvement in Iraq and Afghanistan. The Department of State would take the lead on developing this system in collaboration with the Departments of Defense and Homeland Security.

Identify a centralized location for processing, integration, and adjustment

We recommend that once approved, SIV holders be processed and prepared in a single staging location prior to placement in the US. Using Guam as a staging area was identified as one of the best practices for resettlement from previous experiences with the Vietnamese and Kurds. Guam assisted the refugees by focusing on preparing them for resettlement in the US. It also allowed for more efficient interagency coordination as well as more effective public-private cooperation. The benefits of centralized processing and preparation cannot be overstated.

From the SIV holder's perspective, attention was solely focused on preparing them and their families for arrival in the US. Creating a single staging location allows SIV holders and their families who have been cleared to be moved to a safe location while the remainder of the paperwork is processed. During this time, they can receive education on language, culture, and customs. The goal would be to help the SIV holder and his family be better prepared for a new life once they arrive.

From the government's perspective, collaboration and coordination is more effective when groups are able to work in the same physical space. The current Iraq/Afghanistan SIV holders do not have the centralized coordination of agencies that previously resettled allies did. As a consequence, the SIV holders and their families are not well served. A single processing location allows the government agencies and Volags to conduct a more thorough evaluation of the SIV holder's needs, skills, and goals and thereby work collaboratively to make better decisions regarding placement. To accomplish this, Congress should direct that resettlement of future SIV holders begin through a single staging location.

Develop a separate immigration status from and enhanced benefits beyond the current refugee status

Foreign nationals who work for and with the US and are targeted due to that relationship need to be provided a unique legal status different from other refugees and enhanced resettlement assistance beyond that of a refugee. The current resettlement benefits for SIV holders mirror that of other refugees with only minor exceptions. A foreign national who serves with, works for, risks their life, and in some cases dies for the goals and foreign policy of the US should be given benefits above and beyond that of other refugees. In order to create additional resettlement benefits for SIV holders, Congressional legislation and funding is required.

Grant benefits to killed and wounded foreign nationals

Death benefits should be afforded to family members in the same manner that a US soldier's family is provided when a service member dies while on active duty. Currently, there are no benefits for Iraqis and Afghans who are wounded or killed in battle while working for the US. In addition to providing death benefits, wounded foreign hires who are eligible for the SIV should be fast tracked into the SIV selection process. This also requires Congressional legislation and funding.

Develop best practices from the Vietnamese and Kurdish experience

Federal, state, and local Volags should study how the Vietnamese and Kurdish community centers and groups functioned to understand how to better support the adjustment and integration of current SIV holders. Volags will never have the background and knowledge possessed by foreign nationals from the originating country and we acknowledge that replicating the work of an organically created organization would be extremely challenging. However, Volags have much to learn about what SIV holders from Iraq and Afghanistan need to successfully adjust and achieve self-sufficiency. For current SIV holders, state agencies and local Volags should specifically reach out to some of the organizations listed above as well as local ethnic Iraqi or Afghan serving organizations. Locally run mutual aid societies should also be provided with grants to fund their efforts to support SIV holders and their families.

Federal agencies would also benefit from reviewing the lessons learned from the Vietnamese and Kurdish evacuations and resettlement experiences. The best tools to capture past events and shortcomings in the government are Government Accountability Office (GAO) reports and the Center for Army Lessons Learned (CALL). These organizations have rich material and capture relevant stories that would close the knowledge gap that occurs over time and with administration and organization changeover.

Use the National Guard to enhance network and community integration

We recommend that the Guard develop a state level position and duty description for a SIV coordinator. The National Guards have a clear and influential role to play in assisting the resettlement of SIV holders. National Guard units have established a powerful networking capability. The citizen soldiers live throughout the state, are employed in a variety of jobs, and can provide a network and community upon arrival for SIV holders. In the case of Iraq and Afghanistan, many of the Guard members have served with SIV holders. Given that the US presence in these countries is likely to continue, these relationships will continue to build. The National Guard's SIV coordinator would be responsible for organizing a local network of National Guard members who would assist with integration and adjustment, and provide a local network of friendship that many current SIV holders lack. This would supplement existing support for SIV holders and their families. The Guard SIV coordinator would liaise with public and private resettlement agencies to be alerted about SIV arrivals in order to activate the local network. It is possible that additional funding by states and the federal government may be needed to pay for the coordinator and the work required to effectively support SIV holders.

Holistically evaluate the individual before resettlement

The SIV resettlement process must holistically evaluate the needs, abilities, and goals of the individual SIV holder. In addition, SIV holders should be resettled with either a pre-identified contact or a network of family or friends. Currently, the SIV holder's skills, individual situation, or potential is not a major factor in the resettlement. For example, SIV holders with a fishing background or fishery skills are not encouraged to settle or considered for settlement along the coast. Instead, the federal government pushes out arrivals to the national agencies which then contact the states. States agree upon a yearly quota and will accept or decline based upon the quota. No consideration is given about whether the location of settlement is appropriate for the individual SIV holder or family. If the goal of refugee settlement generally is developing self-sufficiency, ignoring the individual's needs, abilities, and goals effectively defeats the purpose.

This would not be a radically new policy. The US government provided significantly more support to cultivate existing skill sets amongst Cuban refugees until the favored refugee status ended under President Obama. This included funding to retrain professionals and postgraduate certification of physicians. In addition, the US government funded special projects at the University of Miami to develop policies and programs that would most effectively assist Cuban refugees with utilizing their existing skills or developing new skills. This greatly facilitated the economic, social, and political integration of Cuban exiles.[1] We recommend that the same efforts and an equitable level of funding be extended to SIV holders from Afghanistan and Iraq.

To accomplish this, the DoS, HHS, and national Volags must change the decision-making process. Rather than placing SIV holders randomly across the states, the process should determine the best place for the specific family given the skills, contacts, desires, goals, and healthcare needs of the individual or family. With the investment of time and effort, SIV holders will be better equipped to meet the self-sufficiency goal in the INA. Implementing this recommendation would be more effective if coupled with the previous recommendation of

---

[1] Daniels, *Guarding the golden door*

single staging location outside of the SIV holder's country of origin. However, even if Congress does not direct federal agencies to create a single processing location, DoS and HHS should develop policies and procedures to settle SIV holders in a manner that increases the opportunity for self-sufficiency by taking into account the skills, needs, and goals the individual and their family bring with them.

Resettle in states with the best medical support structure for immigrants

SIV holders should not be resettled in states that have not expanded Medicaid to cover adults under 65 years old with income up to 133% of the federal poverty level as funded through the Affordable Care Act (ACA). Currently, SIV holders are provided with eight months of medical benefits that states bill to HHS. In states without Medicaid expansion, the SIV holder loses access to medical insurance unless he obtains employer-provided insurance.

We believe that it is shameful to recruit and employ a foreign national to work on behalf of the US, who is then forced to flee because of that relationship, and then drop access to medical care after eight months. To accomplish this, the DoS and HHS would be required to create a resettlement policy that favors ACA states.

Properly integrate immigrants into the medical system

In order to provide appropriate and timely care, SIV holders should be assigned to a primary care provider and dentist as part of the resettlement process. More explicit training and ongoing support in the navigating the US medical care system also needs to be provided upon arrival. The Western medical system is highly complicated for English speaking native-born US citizens. It is much more so for foreign nationals who are unfamiliar with the system or who do not speak English. The disadvantage is exacerbated by lack of familiarity with the US medical care system. While SIV holders themselves speak English well, their wives or children may not be English language proficient when they arrive. In addition, lack of transportation also makes accessing medical care difficult, especially when settled in suburban or rural areas. All of this costs the US taxpayer and the medical system overall more in the long term. SIV holders who receive support in understanding and working through the complications of the US medical care system are more likely to use it, thus preventing costly emergencies.

In addition, to navigating a complex medical system, there currently is a significant gap in the medical assistance provided. This is simply unacceptable for those who have been displaced because of their support of US foreign policy goals. A primary care physician and dentist needs to be identified for every single SIV holder and their family as part of the resettlement process. Once the SIV holder has a primary point of contact for medical and dental appointments, the staff and doctors can follow through and ensure that the SIV holders and their families do not get lost in the system. One cost efficient way to accomplish this would be to make SIV holders from Iraq and Afghanistan eligible for medical care through the US Department of Veterans Affairs (VA). Payment should still come through the current medical insurance process, but VA medical centers, where available, provide excellent and efficient medical care.

From a security perspective, foreign nationals who are resettled in the US are often marginalized, and are socially and culturally isolated. In various ways, they are vulnerable to domestic recruitment to radicalized ideologies. Undiagnosed or untreated emotional and cognitive challenges can make SIV holders or their family members susceptible to radicalization. Providing proper medical and support services to those who are understandably traumatized, or those who feel unwelcome or lonely due to culture shock, can mitigate the potential influence of terrorist groups. To accomplish this, Congress will need to appropriate funding for medical care. Congress would also need to pass legislation to extend eligibility to VA medical care services to SIV holders whose resettlement was caused by their work with the US government in US military interventions. DoS and HHS will also need to add this task to future grants to resettlement agencies.

Enhance transportation assistance

In order for a SIV holder to reasonably achieve self-sufficiency, a car donation or loan program needs to be established. Currently, the only transportation assistance provided in the INA and ORR regulations is targeted at getting refugees to job training or job interviews. This is simply not enough. SIV holders come here without credit and in most cases without the money for a decent car. Given that efficient and affordable public transportation is lacking throughout most the US, SIV holders must forfeit many jobs that are not within walking distance, hindering their ability to earn a self-sufficient wage.

Congress should either increase funds to the existing resettlement assistance package or create tax incentives to citizens or businesses that donate cars to resettlement agencies. Alternatively, loan guarantee programs with reasonable repayment structures should also be considered. Establishing a vehicle program would be a wise investment in the SIV holder and allow them to adjust, integrate, and achieve self-sufficiency more effectively.

Add transferability of assistance across state lines

Assistance for SIV holders should be nationalized in order to support the mobility that may be necessary to achieve self-sufficiency. Currently, resettlement assistance is tied to the original state of resettlement and is non-transferable simply because of current billing procedures between states, Volags, and the federal granting agencies. When a SIV holder resettles in one state, the state will bill the federal government for the full eight months of medical assistance upon arrival. If the SIV holder receives a job offer in another state, he risks losing his medical assistance if he accepts the job.

The lack of transferability of resettlement assistance is another unnecessary hurdle for SIV holders. SIV arrivals should be registered in a database that is accessible by federal and state officials. HHS and the Department of State can implement this change without Congressional legislation. They will also need to develop an interoperable tracking system to make transferring payments across state lines efficient. This recommendation does require states and Volags to upgrade to a national system.

Chapter 7

Conclusion

Since the 1970s, the United States has evacuated and resettled foreign nationals who have worked for the US and whose lives have been threatened because of that relationship four times. The evacuation and resettlement of the South Vietnamese in the mid-1970s and the Iraqi Kurds in the mid-1990s was hastily planned. Nevertheless, it worked to bring US allies to safety and integrate them into their new communities. The same cannot be said for current Special Immigrant Visa (SIV) holders from Iraq and Afghanistan.

The successes and challenges in each case of evacuation and resettlement were heavily influenced by the political, economic, and socio-cultural context of each time. The evacuation of South Vietnamese allies benefitted from significant political support, starting with President Ford's argument that the US had a moral obligation to evacuate and resettle them in the US. The US was experiencing significant economic stress during this time. Nevertheless, the South Vietnamese refugees found a labor market niche that did not compete with US Americans, especially White Americans. They also benefitted from lower urban housing costs which allowed them to settle in pre-existing urban ethnic enclaves near public transportation as well as social and medical services. The ability to resettle as a community also facilitated mutual aid and support, which was a key factor in their successful integration.

Politically, the Iraqi Kurds benefitted from a relatively disinterested and intentionally uninformed public. President Clinton decided to quietly evacuate Kurdish allies and process them in Guam in order to keep it out of the public eye during the 1996 presidential campaign. This decision was tacitly supported by his rival candidate. The evacuated Kurds were generally highly educated and were able to plug into a strong economy with greater ease than the average refugee. Like the South Vietnamese before them, Kurds were resettled in pre-existing Kurdish communities, especially in and around Nashville, Tennessee. The mutual aid and support from previous immigrants significantly contributed to their successful resettlement and integration.

Unfortunately, for Iraqi and Afghan SIV holders, the political, economic, and socio-cultural context is much more challenging. There has historically been strong bipartisan support for the SIV program in Congress despite deep polarization between the two political parties. Support for the SIV program was also strong under Presidents Bush and Obama. President Trump, however, is strongly opposed to resettling any refugees. He attempted to put a moratorium on the SIV program entirely and only relented after intense criticism by the public,

Congress, and the military. The US economy is also making it difficult for Iraqi and Afghan refugees to achieve the goal of economic self-sufficiency. The global economic recession had started just when the SIV program began to receive applications. It also does not help that SIV holders are being resettled randomly across the country. The lack of mutual aid from a community who speaks the same language and shares cultural norms and traditions is making it more difficult than necessary for SIV holders to integrate into US society. In addition, widespread anti-Muslim bias and overt discrimination, as well as violence, is making an already challenging resettlement process more difficult.

In our analysis, we find that the organizations involved in the domestic resettlement process are doing a number of things well. There are also significant improvements that are needed to better support current SIV holders. We find that states that fund an office for a refugee resettlement coordinator are more invested in operating effective resettlement programs. State resettlement agencies and the non-profit voluntary agencies (Volags) that do the on-the-ground work are largely coordinating well. Volags are increasingly working more closely with the communities where they are resettling SIV holders. This allows the Volags to make better decisions about where to resettle SIV holders with particular needs and helps the communities more effectively welcome and support their new residents. National advocacy organizations are providing much needed assistance to bridge the gaps between what the federal and state grants pay for and what SIV holders need. Importantly, they are also lobbying to ensure that the SIV program retains support, at least in Congress. Where possible, SIV holders are providing mutual aid and support just as previous groups did.

What is making resettlement, integration, and economic self-sufficiency challenging is the limited assistance packages available to SIV holders. There simply is not enough financial assistance and there is not enough time provided in the law to facilitate sustained integration and dignified financial independence. Operational constraints, specifically the lack of transferability of assistance across state lines, makes effective support of SIV holders unnecessarily difficult. On the whole, resettlement agencies and Volags also do not pay enough attention to the individual needs, goals, and potential of each SIV holder and his family when making placement decisions.

Above all, the random, or at least unplanned, placement of current SIV holders across the country has significant impacts on the ability of the SIV holder and his family to achieve economic self-sufficiency and integration into a community. The location of resettlement affects everything from access to jobs, medical care, social services, and affordable transportation to culturally appropriate mutual aid and support. While there is some coordination happening between Volags and local communities, it is not a common practice. As a result, it is not unusual for SIV holders and their families to be placed in communities that are unprepared, and potentially unwilling, to support their successful resettlement.

Our recommendations are intended to support the ability of the SIV holder to achieve economic self-sufficiency as well as successfully integrate into the US. Some of these recommendations require changes in the Immigration and Nationality Act (INA). Others simply require more funding. Many can be pursued under existing statutory authorization and funding. We believe that SIV applications from Iraqis and Afghans who work with Special Operations Forces in the field should have priority over applications from places where the insurgent threat is not as severe. In addition, a centralized out-of-country processing location to prepare for resettlement is a good practice from the Vietnamese and Kurdish experience that should be revived for SIV holders. The federal and state agencies, as well as the Volags, have a lot to learn from the Vietnamese and Kurdish resettlement. They should undertake a collaborative analysis to identify the best practices that should be replicated for current SIV holders.

SIV holders are being evacuated from Iraq and Afghanistan because of their work in support of US foreign policy goals. For this reason, we believe that a different immigration status separate from humanitarian refugee is warranted. We argue that SIV holders should receive assistance that aligns with the benefits provided to US military veterans. Further, because SIV holders often work closely with National Guard units deployed to Afghanistan and Iraq, we believe there is an opportunity to collaborate with the National Guard to provide a social support network that would facilitate employment as well as community integration.

Of particular importance is ending the "Resettlement Lottery" practice in the placement of SIV holders.[1] SIV holders should only be placed in locations where they have the best chance of achieving economic self-sufficiency and living dignified lives. We argue that SIV holders should only be resettled in states that have expanded access to Medicaid under the Affordable Care Act. SIV holders should not be placed in locations where they will lose access to necessary medical care because the state refuses to take advantage of federal funding to provide medical care to adults who traditionally do not qualify for Medicaid. Further, greater effort to assist SIV holders to effectively use available medical care is needed.

In addition, SIV holders need to be more holistically evaluated before placement. Some places will be more appropriate for unmarried SIV holders than those with spouses and children. In particular, SIV holders with families can integrate more successfully if settled near others from the same language and cultural group. SIV holders with particular goals and skills should be settled in places where those goals

---

[1] International Rescue Committee, *Iraqi refugees in the United States*

can be met and where their skills would contribute to the communities in which they are placed. Taking into account the different needs, life goals, and potential of the SIV holder and his family would more effectively achieve the goal of self-sufficiency than the current process is doing.

Finally, the transferability of resettlement assistance across state lines is critical. SIV holders should not be compelled to choose between a good job offer in another state and maintaining access to medical care or social support. This is especially the case for SIV holders with dependent family members.

A precarious future for resettled allies under the Trump Administration

As of this writing, the future of the refugee resettlement program is precarious, which will have significant impact on current SIV holders and previously resettled allies. Bipartisan support in Congress appears to be holding.[2] Indeed, in the FY 2017 National Defense Authorization Act (NDAA),[3] Congress increased the annual visa allotment by over 20% through FY 2020. However, the nativist turn in national politics has put the program at risk. President Trump's muscular statism and

---

[2] It is important to note that we completed this book before the November 2018 mid-term elections, which could change the level of bipartisanship on this issue.
[3] The FY 2017 NDAA was passed by Congress with overwhelming bipartisan support in December 2016 and signed into law by President Obama in December 2016.

anti-immigrant rhetoric is not friendly to refugee resettlement, especially for people from predominantly Muslim countries like Iraq and Afghanistan. The appointment of Andrew Veprek, whose view of refugees has been described as "vindictive," to the head the Bureau of Population, Refugees, and Migration raises the possibility that refugee resettlement may be dramatically curtailed under the Trump administration.[4]

It would not be difficult for the Trump administration to thwart the will of Congress on this matter. From 2009 through 2012, Ambassador Eikenberry reduced the issuance of SIVs by 91%. It is not impossible for this to happen again. A slowdown in the issuance of SIVs from Afghanistan is already evident. There has been a 55% decline in SIV arrivals from Afghanistan between the last quarter of 2017 and the first quarter of 2018.[5] It is not yet clear whether this is an intentional slowdown by a rogue executive official, a temporary slowdown because of personnel changes in the Department of State or Department of Homeland Security, or whether it is related to the confusion caused by the many court decisions from the lawsuits challenging President Trump's immigration related executive orders

---

[4] Toosi, N. (2018, March 8). Refugee skeptic lands top State Department refugee job. *Politico*. Retrieved from https://www.politico.com/story/2018/03/08/andrew-veprek-state-department-refugee-admissions-448210

[5] Bureau of Population, Refugees, and Migration. (n.d.). *Admissions & arrivals*. Retrieved from US Department of State: http://www.wrapsnet.org/admissions-and-arrivals/

and proclamations.[6] Nevertheless, given the goal of reducing migration into the US, and particularly from refugees, the reduction in SIV issuances signals a potential policy shift that will be difficult to overcome in the current political climate.

Additional pressures on the SIV program may also come from the reduction in the cap on refugees for FY 2018. The 1980 Refugee Act sets the refugee limit at 50,000 per year. It also includes a provision to allow the president to determine the number of refugee admissions in any fiscal year as "justified by humanitarian concerns or is otherwise in the national interest."[7] The annual ceiling has never been lower than 67,000.[8] For the first time ever, President Trump reduced the cap on the number of refugees to below the congressionally authorized cap.[9] The FY 2018 ceiling was set to 45,000. This is almost a 60% decline from the previous cap of 110,000 set for FY 2017.[10] This reduction will put significant pressure on the Iraqi SIV program, which is likely to run out of SIV allotments at some point during FY 2018. If this

---

[6] Specifically Executive Order 13780 and Presidential Proclamation 9645.

[7] The Refugee Act §207(a)(2). See also Reimers, *An unintended reform*

[8] The Economist. (2017, August 31). *The roots of Afghanistan's tribal tensions.* Retrieved from https://www.economist.com/blogs/economist-explains/2017/08/economist-explains-21. The FY 2017 ceiling reported in the MPI chart as of May 12, 2018 is incorrect. The ceiling was set at 110,000 by President Barack Obama in September 2016. See https://www.state.gov/j/prm/releases/docsforcongress/261956.htm.

[9] The List Project to Resettle Iraqi Allies, *Home*

[10] US Department of State. (2016, September 15). *Proposed Refugee Admissions for Fiscal Year 2017.* Retrieved from https://www.state.gov/j/prm/releases/docsforcongress/261956.htm

happens, the only option for Iraqi allies whose lives are threatened because of their work with the US government is the US Refugee Admissions Program. Unless Congress steps in to renew the Iraqi SIV program, Iraqi allies whose lives are threatened because they work with the US government will find it increasingly difficult to obtain a visa.

An even more problematic trend is the Trump administration's indiscriminate targeting of immigrants for deportation. Immigration and Customs Enforcement (ICE) has been targeting immigrants with old deportation orders and conducting raids and roundups in Vietnamese and Kurdish communities. In many cases, ICE has targeted people convicted of minor crimes committed more than a decade ago. In the case of Vietnamese and Iraqi refugees, many of the people swept up in these raids have been detained for several months without a bond hearing.[11]

---

[11] Hamama v. Adducci, (2018 E.D. Mich.). Retrieved from https://www.gpo.gov/fdsys/pkg/USCOURTS-mied-2_17-cv-11910/pdf/USCOURTS-mied-2_17-cv-11910-5.pdf; Johannes, C. (2017, October 6). US Kurds face detention, deportation as Trump cracks down on immigration. *Rudaw*. Retrieved from http://www.rudaw.net/english/kurdistan/10062017; Sisk, C. (2017, June 9). At least 6 former Kurdish refugees face deportation amid what activists describe as a sweep. *Nashville Public Radio*. Retrieved from http://nashvillepublicradio.org/post/least-6-former-kurdish-refugees-face-deportation-amid-what-activists-describe-sweep#stream/0; Schmidt, S. (2018, March 1). Vietnamese immigrants are stuck in limbo, detained indefinitely, lawsuit says. *The Washington Post*. Retrieved from https://www.washingtonpost.com/news/morning-

The Trump administration also appears to be willing to violate the terms of a 2008 Memorandum of Understanding with Vietnam in which the US agreed not to deport South Vietnamese refugees who arrived in the US prior to 1995. This agreement functioned to protect Vietnamese refugees who supported the former South Vietnamese government. The current communist government in Vietnam refuses to accept individuals they assume would be "destabilizing elements."[12] Previously, non-citizens who would otherwise be deportable but whose country of birth either refused to accept them or were unable to guarantee their safety were allowed to live freely as long as they agreed to be regularly monitored. As of this writing, ICE is currently detaining at least 40 Vietnamese refugees, some for over a year, and reportedly plans to hold them until Vietnam agrees to accept them back. Class action lawsuits have been filed on behalf of detained

mix/wp/2018/03/01/vietnamese-immigrants-are-stuck-in-limbo-detained-indefinitely-lawsuit-says; Levin, S. (2018, March 3). Detained and divided: how the US turned on Vietnamese refugees. *The Guardian*. Retrieved from https://www.theguardian.com/us-news/2018/mar/03/vietnamese-refugees-immigration-us-detention; Hayoun, M. (2018, March 7). The Trump administration is failing to uphold its commitments to Vietnamese refugees. *Pacific Standard*. Retrieved from https://psmag.com/social-justice/the-trump-administration-is-failing-to-uphold-its-commitments-to-vietnamese-refugees
[12] Pearson, J. (2018, April 12). US seeks to deport thousands of Vietnamese protected by treaty: former ambassador. *Reuters*. Retrieved from https://www.reuters.com/article/us-usa-vietnam-deportees/u-s-seeks-to-deport-thousands-of-vietnamese-protected-by-treaty-former-ambassador-idUSKBN1HJ0OU; Sanchez, T. (2018, April 6). Former ambassador to Vietnam: Trump wanted me to send back refugees. *The Mercury News*. Retrieved from https://www.mercurynews.com/2018/04/06/former-ambassador-to-vietnam-trump-wanted-me-to-send-back-refugees/

Vietnamese refugees and similar lawsuits have been filed for at least 100 Iraqis in similar situations. Community advocates argue that the indefinite detention is part of an attempt to pressure Vietnam and eight other countries to accept deportees that they have officially stated they are unwilling to accept.[13]

This aggressive effort to deport Vietnamese and Kurdish refugees also puts the entire mission in Iraq and Afghanistan at risk. If the Trump administration is successful in deporting refugees from previous conflicts that the US had promised to protect, it will reduce the willingness of foreign nationals to work for the US government in Iraq and Afghanistan and significantly undermine the mission in both countries.

Another worrisome development is the administrative burdens and roll back of the Affordable Care Act (ACA). While Congress failed to repeal the ACA in 2017, the Trump administration has used its executive discretion in ways that will allow states to limit access to Medicaid, reduce subsidies and thereby increase the cost of medical insurance, or otherwise threaten the stability of the medical insurance market. Some states have responded by strengthening their own health insurance laws or expanding access to medical insurance. Other states are taking advantage of the opportunity to reduce their Medicaid rolls

---

[13] Schmidt, *Vietnamese immigrants are stuck in limbo*; Pearson, *US seeks to deport thousands of Vietnamese*; Hayoun, *The Trump administration is failing*

even further.[14] SIV holders and their families who are placed in states taking full advantage of the administrative roll backs will find themselves with even less access to much needed medical and mental health care.

Our moral obligation

We cannot overstate the significance of the SIV program and how important it is that every effort is made to make resettlement successful. It is literally a matter of life and death. One of our interviewees told us about someone he knew who lost his life because of a botched resettlement process. The SIV holder and family arrived in the US with two small children. Their landlord never received the check for the rent from the resettlement agency and filed for an eviction. The SIV holder did not understand the importance of the letters from the municipal court and the resettlement agency was not providing support on this matter. After several months, the court granted an eviction. The SIV holder found himself with an outstanding warrant for unpaid rent, no credit, and no money. This family was

---

[14] Brownstein, R. (2018, March 8). The health-care gap between red and blue America. *The Atlantic*. Retrieved from https://www.theatlantic.com/politics/archive/2018/03/obamacare-trump/555131/; Levitt, L. (2018, January 5). The Trump administration's hidden attacks on the Affordable Care Act. *The Washington Post*. Retrieved from https://www.washingtonpost.com/opinions/the-trump-administrations-hidden-attacks-on-the-affordable-care-act/2018/01/05/bd7002da-f237-11e7-97bf-bba379b809ab_story.html?utm_term=.741f2f7c3d07

forced to move into a homeless shelter. Unable to find a job, he became depressed. He eventually returned to Afghanistan with his family, was found by the Taliban, and killed.

In 1975, President Ford argued that the United States had a "special obligation" to welcome our South Vietnamese allies whose lives were threatened because of their support of US foreign policy. We argue that the moral obligation to SIV holders from Iraq and Afghanistan is at least as great. The Iraqis and Afghans who worked with US-led coalition forces put their faith in our promise to transform their countries. They continue to risk their lives and the safety of their families for US foreign policy goals. They would not be in the position of fleeing their own country but for the US-led military intervention.

SIV holders are not simply humanitarian refugees. They are creations of US foreign policy. They have risked their lives and the lives of their families; they have bled and died with and for our men and women in uniform. Those who make it to the US for their own safety are forced to leave behind their family, the only community they know, and their social standing. They deserve a status worthy of their sacrifice.

The current process of refugee resettlement almost automatically places SIV holders in a lower socio-economic position despite the skills and talents they have to offer. We do them and ourselves a disservice by forcing them to live without a social support system in often unprepared (and increasingly hostile) communities. Coercing SIV holders to accept substandard jobs that do not take advantage of their skills or take into account their goals is misguided at best. Compelling them to live in states that cannot provide adequate medical, mental health, or social services is cruel given the debt we owe to SIV holders and their families.

When the US recruits local hires in Iraq and Afghanistan, we explicitly and implicitly pledge to protect them as employees. When all else fails, the SIV is there to safeguard those whose lives were threatened. The current policy and practice of resettling our allies is shamefully inadequate given the promises made and our duty to protect those whose sacrifice was so great.

APPENDICES

LAWS, POLICIES, & ORGANIZATIONAL STRUCTURE

During 20th century military conflicts, the US has resettled foreign nationals four times, both after and during conflicts. First, the fall of Vietnam brought a wave of Vietnamese soldiers and civilians. In the second resettlement, Iraqi Kurds working for UN-flagged forces in northern Iraq. Most recently, with a growing humanitarian crisis in Iraq and Afghanistan, and US credibility under question, the US government formulated another ad hoc program known as the Special Immigrant Visa (SIV) in 2006. Appendix A describes the development of the legal authority for evacuation and eventual resettlement used in each of those conflicts.

The processing and resettlement of refugees and Special Immigrant Visa (SIV) holders spans multiple U.S. government agencies at the federal and state level as well as non-governmental organizations. These agencies are responsible for identifying immigrants, conducting background checks, administrative processing, identifying resettlement locations in the U.S., transportation to the U.S., housing, educational courses, and job placement. The organizational structure, funding model, and operational process have not changed in any significant way since the evacuation of South Vietnam. Appendix B describes the organizational structure of refugee resettlement.

Appendix A

Historical and current laws & policies

Vietnam

Before the fall of Saigon in 1975, the Ford administration was left with the incredible responsibility of creating and enacting a policy for Vietnamese allies who would be targeted after the fall of Saigon. The Ford administration viewed the loss of Vietnam and the eventual massive exodus of Vietnamese allies as a moral and ethical obligation.

With creative interpretation of the Immigration and Naturalization Act of 1965 (INA), the administration accepted an initial 130,000 Vietnamese under the humanitarian parole status. Humanitarian parole is a little known but expedient path found in the Immigration and Naturalization Act of 1965 to quickly grant entry into the US.[1] Parole status may be granted:

> *To anyone applying for admission into the United States based on urgent humanitarian reasons or if there is a significant public benefit, or for a period of time that*

---

[1] Scanlan & Loescher, *Calculated Kindness*; US Customs and Immigration Service. (n.d.). *Immigration and Nationality Act*. Retrieved from https://www.uscis.gov/ilink/docView/SLB/HTML/SLB/act.html.

corresponds with the length of the emergency or

humanitarian situation.[2]

The Ford administration interpreted this language as supporting the evacuation of Vietnamese allies. The INA provided President Ford with the authorization to do this temporary action. Despite reservations on the part of many, Congress did not object because they wanted to avoid thousands of US allies being imprisoned, tortured, and killed because of their allegiance to the US.[3] Ford's action injected some level of compassion, heroism, and humanity into an otherwise-depressing narrative.

Soon after, Congress passed the Indochinese Migration and Refugee Assistance Act in order to properly operate and administer the admission and resettlement of Vietnamese immigrants.[4] This law provided funding to the Department of State and the Department of Health, Education, and Welfare for evacuation and resettlement. It also authorized an Interagency Task Force (IATF) of 12 federal government agencies to collaborate on the evacuation and resettlement

---

[2] US Customs and Immigration Service, *Immigration and Nationality Act*
[3] Scanlan & Loescher, *Calculated Kindness*
[4] Although the law applied to allies from Laos and Cambodia, the majority of allies processed and resettled in the US were Vietnamese. See Scanlan & Loescher, *Calculated Kindness*.

of Vietnamese allies and their families.[5]

For the first time in US history, military and civilian agencies arrived in Guam for reception of what would be hundreds of thousands of South Vietnamese. Neither the military nor the resettlement agencies had ever operated or managed a resettlement on this scale.[6] Over the course of several months, South Vietnamese, by ship and aircraft, arrived in Guam for eventual resettlement to the US.

As a member of the IATF, the Department of Defense (DoD) was given enormous duties and responsibilities. The Department of Defense was tasked to operate reception centers, located in the Pacific and the United States, transport the Vietnamese immigrants, and provide for the shelter, meals, medical support, and the security of the immigrants. As DoD took on the service support and operational responsibilities, the other 11 agencies focused on the processing and resettlement of the Vietnamese immigrants.[7] Andersen Air Force Base

---

[5] Marsh, *Socioeconomic status of Indochinese refugees in the United States.* Members of the IATF included Departments of: State; Defense; Justice; Health, Education, and Welfare; Transportation; Treasury; Labor; Interior; and Housing and Urban Development. In addition, the IATF included representatives of the US Agency for International Development; the US Information Agency; the Central Intelligence Agency; the Office of Management and Budget; and the Immigration and Naturalization Service. See US Department of Defense, *Operation New Life/New Arrivals.*
[6] Paradise, K. G. (1977). *From Vietnam to America: A chronicle of the Vietnamese immigration to the United States.* Boulder, CO: Westview Press.
[7] US Department of Defense, *Operation Pacific Haven wraps up humanitarian efforts*

in Guam became the obvious geographic, political, and legally suitable staging ground for the Vietnamese. In this unincorporated territory of the US, the immigration status of a parolee/refugee could be adjusted, as the Vietnamese were technically on US soil. Geographically, military ships and aircraft could quickly shuttle those fleeing. And politically, the chaos which ensued during the initial resettlement phases would occur outside the continental US. A majority of the 130,000 Vietnamese who were evacuated and resettled through the Indochinese refugee program went through Guam on their way to the US.[8]

In 1977, Congress passed Public Law 95-145 which allowed those Vietnamese (and others) who were granted parole status to apply for legal permanent residency after residing in the US for two years. Further, the law expedited citizenship for all Vietnamese who entered the US under the status of parole.[9]

Iraqi Kurds

Much as in Vietnam, the Iraqi Kurds supporting US forces and operating out of U.N. bases in Northern Iraq became a target of Saddam Hussein. With few alternative options for their security, the executive and legislative branch once again took advantage of the

---

[8] Paradise, *From Vietnam to America*
[9] Marsh, *Socioeconomic status of Indochinese refugees in the United States*

flexibility in the INA and Andersen Air Force Base in Guam. The depth and breadth of the resettlement of Iraqi Kurds from northern Iraq pale was not nearly as large or as fraught as the evacuation of Vietnamese allies. However, the speed and decision making by policymakers was unprecedented.

Under 8 USC §1158, asylum is granted to those physically in the US or who are brought to the US. In order to grant Kurds asylum status, the US government chartered flights out of US bases in Turkey to Guam, an unincorporated US territory. Kurds departed Iraq for Turkey as refugees and arrived in Guam as asylum seekers. Once in Guam, the Kurds were eligible for asylum under the Immigration and Naturalization Act.[10]

Operation Pacific Haven was established on September 16, 1996, and lasted 218 days. In total, 6,600 Kurdish evacuees were processed through Andersen Air Force Base with the US as their final destination. This effort consisted of 1,600 military and interagency personnel. Once again, Guam served the needs of allies who were targeted due to their relationship with the US government.

In addition to meeting the immediate needs of the newly arrived

---

[10] Jones, J. (2017). Operation Provide Comfort: A forgotten mission with possible lessons for Syria. *Foreign Policy*. Retrieved from http://foreignpolicy.com/2017/02/06/operation-provide-comfort-a-forgotten-mission-with-possible-lessons-for-syria/

refugees, Guam served as a special immigration-processing center for the Kurds. The Immigration and Naturalization Service was responsible for processing applicants into the federal immigration database and conducting background checks, while the Department of Health and Human Services was responsible for medical screening and matching evacuees with volunteer agencies to be resettled in the US. At that time, a typical asylum process for one person ranged in duration from six months to one year. While on Guam, the interagency task force was able to simplify the asylum process, shortening the average time for an asylum hearing to 90-120 days.[11] In addition, Kurds were provided with medical care, food, housing, and a basic education in language, customs, and culture to facilitate resettlement.[12]

Iraq and Afghanistan

The Global War on Terror resulted in the third resettlement of foreign nationals. This time, it was in Iraq and Afghanistan where those who worked for and with US forces who were targeted because of that relationship. The US Department of Homeland Security, an agency that had not existed in prior resettlements, would add a new bureaucratic layer to the resettlement process. Also a first, the resettlement of foreign nationals through the country of Guam was no

---

[11] US Department of Defense, *Operation Pacific Haven wraps up humanitarian efforts*
[12] Ibid

longer an option.[13] The US government again used creative interpretations of the INA, but also created new legal tools to resettle foreign nationals through a more formal process than experienced with the evacuation and resettlement of the Vietnamese and Iraqi Kurds. The description of the laws described here is drawn from Andorra Bruno's Congressional Research Service report *Iraqi and Afghan Special Immigrant,* unless otherwise noted.[14]

The Special Immigrant Visa (SIV) was created to admit and resettle Iraqi and Afghan foreign nationals who worked directly for and on behalf of US forces, or International Security Forces (ISAF) in subsequent amendments, as part of the Global War on Terror. The definition of the Special Immigrant can be found in Section 101(a)(27) of the INA, as amended in 1965 and 1990. The categories of Special Immigrants is an assortment of foreign nationals ranging from former employees of the Panama Canal to medical doctors to broadcasters to religious workers. There is no subsection within 101(a)(27) specific to Iraq or Afghanistan. The SIV program described here are creations of several National Defense Authorization Acts.

In addition to the specific eligibility criteria set in the laws creating these programs, the guidelines for admissibility mirror those applied to

---

[13] Attempts to determine why Guam could not be used were unsuccessful. Knowledgeable officials interviewed did not provide a specific reason why resettling through Guam was no longer an option.

[14] Bruno, *Iraqi and Afghan Special Immigrant Visa programs*

other immigrant visas. Applicants must not have a criminal record and must pass a health examination. The only exception with SIVs compared to immigrant categories is that SIV applicants are exempt from the public charge exclusion criteria. During a typical immigration visa application, applicants must demonstrate they personally have sufficient funds or have an economically sufficient support structure in the US, otherwise the applicant is deemed inadmissible. SIV applicants cannot be denied due to risk of becoming a public charge. This is largely because there is a support structure and assistance package for asylees, refugees, and special immigrant visa holders that is not provided to other visa classes.

The SIV for Iraqis and Afghans is broken down into three programs. The first program, first enacted in Section 1059 of the National Defense Authorization Act (NDAA) for Fiscal Year 2006, was enacted in 2006 and amended in 2007. It was established specifically and only for Iraqi and Afghan interpreters. The second program, Section 1244 of the National Defense Authorization Act for Fiscal Year 2008, was established for Iraqis who worked for or on behalf of the US government. The third program, Title VI of Omnibus Appropriations Act 2009 was established to replicate the Iraqi program for Afghans who worked for or on behalf of the US government.

Although there are technically three programs, there are really are only two categories of SIVs. The first category is for Iraqis and

Afghans who served as interpreters or translators. The second category is for Afghans and Iraqis who worked for or on behalf of the US government or ISAF members. The first category is much clearer cut than the latter, as an interpreter or translator is a specific position with defined duties. By contrast, the definition of someone who "worked for or on behalf of the US government" is extremely broad. For example, an Iraqi or Afghan who accepted a grant from the US government to dig a well technically is working on behalf of the US government.

The laws authorizing the Iraq and Afghan SIV also formalized the application process to a much greater degree than seen with the Vietnamese or Iraqi Kurds. The involvement of the Department of Homeland Security has also added a layer of complexity to an already complex and uncertain process.

Iraqi and Afghan Interpreters

Section 1059 of the National Defense Authorization Act of FY 2006 authorized Afghan and Iraqi interpreters to be resettled in the US. The initial cap was limited to 50 interpreters per year total for both Iraq and Afghanistan. Eligible applicants must have worked for or on behalf of the US government for at least one year and obtain a written letter of recommendation from the Chief of Mission. This law was narrowly tailored to issue visas and resettle interpreters who worked directly for US military forces. Congress amended Section 1059 in 2007 to increase the number of applicants from 50 to 500 annually and expanded the employment eligibility from US military forces to include Iraqis and Afghans under Chief of Mission Authority (see Table A.1).

The Chief of Mission (COM) is designated by the Ambassador in the respective country and is typically assigned to a US State Department employee. The authorization of COM expanded authority beyond US military hired interpreters and translators. Since the Ambassador was the US government's senior representative in both Iraq and Afghanistan, a majority of Iraq and Afghan interpreters (and other employees) essentially worked for or on behalf of the US Department of State.

Table A.1: Description of the Iraq & Afghan Interpreters SIV program

Law	Year	Eligibility	Visas Available (annual)	Eligibility Criteria	Employment Criteria
§1059 NDAA	2006	Iraqis and Afghans	50	Interpreter/ translator for US military forces	1 year
§1059 NDAA	2007 Amendments	Iraqis and Afghans	500	Interpreter/ translator for US forces Chief of Mission*	1 year

*Chief of Mission Authority is granted by the US Department of State.

As is typical in special immigrant visas, spouses and children are not counted against the cap. SIV holders are treated as refugees and thus are eligible for resettlement assistance from the Department of Health and Human Services, Office of Refugee Resettlement and Department of State's Bureau of Population, Refugee, and Migration. Any visas not issued in a given year could be carried forward to subsequent years.

Iraq Program

Section 1244 of the National Defense Authorization Act for FY 2008 authorized the SIV program for five years (with an expiration at the end of 2013) and represented a long-term investment in the Iraqi SIV program. The criteria and eligibility in Section 1244 were drawn from Section 1059 as amended in 2007. Eligible applicants must have worked for or on behalf of the US government for at least one year on or after March 20th, 2003, demonstrate they are under a serious threat due to their employment, and obtain a written letter of recommendation from the Chief of Mission. The number of visas authorized was capped at 5,000 principal applicants annually with transfer of unissued visas to flow to the next year. An extension of 2,500 visas was authorized in the National Defense Authorization Act for Fiscal Year 2014 (see Table A.2). On September 30th, 2014, the application deadline expired; however, the U.S. Department of State continued to process applications received prior to the deadline.

Table A.2: Description of the Iraq SIV program

Law	Year	Annual Visas Available	Eligibility Criteria	Employment Criteria
§1244 NDAA	2008	5,000	Chief of Mission*	1 year starting on or after 3/20/2003
§1244 NDAA	2014	2,500	Chief of Mission*	1 year starting on or after 3/20/2003

Afghanistan Program

In 2009, Title VI of the Omnibus Appropriation Act of Fiscal Year 2009, also called the Afghan Allies Protection Act of 2009, expanded eligibility to Afghans who have worked by or on behalf of the U.S government in Afghanistan or by the International Security Assistance Force (ISAF) or successor mission. This law replicates the criteria used for the Iraq program; eligible applicants must have worked for or on behalf of the US government for at least one year (with a start date of on or after October 7th, 2001), demonstrate a serious threat due to their employment, and obtain a written letter of recommendation from the Chief of Mission. The Afghan SIV was capped at 1,500 annually from fiscal year 2009 through fiscal 2013 but was increased to 3,000 in fiscal year 2014. Congress has extended the authorization for the program on a yearly basis through the annual National Defense Authorization acts between 2014 and 2017, increasing the caps first to 4,000 and then to 7,000. In 2017, the National Defense Authorization Act for Fiscal Year 2017 authorized 8,500 visas through 2020 (See

Table A.3).

Table A.3: Description of the Afghan SIV program

Law	Years	Annual Visas Available
Omnibus Appropriation Act of FY2009	2009-2013	1,500
National Defense Authorization Act for FY2014	2014	3,000
National Defense Authorization Act for FY2015	2015	4,000
National Defense Authorization Act for FY2016	2016	7,000
National Defense Authorization Act for FY2017	2017-2020	8,500

The Application Process. The application process for the SIV is far more formal and structured compared with the process of past resettlements. SIV applicants navigate a four-step process in order to obtain a SIV and begin the resettlement process. Applicants can expect the processing to take many months. The application process for a Special Immigrant Visa will touch and pass through an impressive number of government agencies, both federal and state, as well as non-profit groups assisting in the resettlement. The process of applying for, receiving, and resettling in the US is led by the US Department of State. The other federal agencies involved in the SIV application and resettlement process include the Department of Homeland Security (DHS), and US Department of State. Applicants are also cleared through various national security agencies. The description of the application process described here is drawn from the US Department of State's website, unless otherwise noted.[15]

In step 1, the initial forms are completed to determine eligibility and establish employment relationships. All SIV applicants, Iraqi and Afghan, must produce letters of recommendation, and complete DHS form I-360 (Petition for Amerasian, Widow(er), or Special Immigrant Visa) to properly identify their category of eligibility, proof of employment, and current citizenship. This form collects basic biographic information that initiates the application process. Since three classifications exist for the SIV under the GWOT, another function of the I-360 is to determine which program the applicant is eligible for. The key deliverables that accompany the form are proof of employment with the US government and a letter of recommendation from a General or Flag Officer or from the Chief of Mission at the US Embassy.

In the early years of the SIV, the US government required a sworn letter, written by the applicant, to state the danger and threat posed that would justify the essential evacuation and resettlement. The threat statement requirement continued as the law expanded and created a class of SIV for Iraqis and Afghans who worked for or on behalf of the US government. The applicant was required to outline the overt threat

---

[15] US Department of State. (2017, Oct). *U.S. Visas*. Retrieved from: https://travel.state.gov/content/visas/en/immigrate/afghans-work-for-us.html

that was made or to highlight statements, phone calls, or letters received by mail. After 2017, the statement of threat is no longer required.

All SIV applications are routed through the United States Customs and Immigration Service (USCIS), Nebraska Service Center (NSC), located in Lincoln, Nebraska. The entire packet is mailed by the applicant to the NSC. Contact with the applicant for additional information or clarification occurs through e-mail. The NSC is the final adjudication authority for SIV applications. Upon approval, the SIVs packet is mailed to the National Visa Center (NVC) in Portsmouth, NH for further processing once the packet is complete, including the completion of required background and security checks.

The second step of the process occurs after the NSC favorably adjudicates the application. During this phase, applicants submit additional documents for background screening. Form DS-260 (Immigrant Visa and Alien Registration Application) is 76 pages long and encompasses the biographical and familial background of the applicant as well as certifying the applicant's intent, will, and purpose for resettling in the US. As a deliverable, the SIV applicant provides a family tree, contact numbers, list of relatives, and other supporting documents, including passport and birth certificate.

Also during this second step, the applicants must elect to receive resettlement benefits. To be eligible for the US Department of State's

Reception and Placement (R&P) Program, applicants must complete the Refugee Benefits Election form DS-0234 and Special Immigrant Visa Biodata form before departing for the US. These forms are not required for resettlement but are necessary if the SIV applicant wants assistance with travel, loans, housing, transportation, or basic resettlement upon arrival to the US. The R&P program provides newly arrived foreign nationals with a support structure in the US and assistance in resettling. Applicants who have family ties in the US and/or wish to settle in a specific location without assistance will not receive the US Department of State's Reception and Placement (R&P) funds. Declining assistance through these initial programs does not reflect on resettlement benefits provided by the Department of Health and Human Services, Office of Refugee Resettlement (HHS/ORR), which offers medical, food stamps, and employment assistance. While the applicant must make choices about resettlement during this step, there is no guarantee that they will be granted the SIV.

The third step occurs once the applicant successfully completes the background and security checks. If an applicant successfully makes it through those checks, the NVC can complete its review and adjudication of the applicant's documents. Once the NVC determines the file is complete, it will schedule the final interview and mail the packet to the embassy for final adjudication. A US Department of State Foreign Service Officer (FSO) at the embassy will conduct the final interview, ensure the packet is complete, conduct an interview face to face, and make a determination to issue or deny the visa. The FSO conducts the interview with the applicant, his/her spouse, and children under 21 years of age. Documents such as birth certificates, marriage certificates, and passports are required to be presented during the interview. Applicants are required to cover the cost of transportation to and from the embassy and pay $205 for each visa application. Upon completion of the interview, further processing can take an additional 60 days.

In the final step of the SIV process, applicants arrive in the US. A multitude of groups and agencies at all levels coordinate the resettlement process. Three programs have been established to manage and fund the resettlement: the US Refugee Admission Program (USRAP), US Department of State's Reception and Placement (R&P) Program, and the International Organization for Migration (IOM). A variety of agencies, both governmental and non-governmental, are involved in the resettlement process. The USRAP is the overarching program that encompasses the security screening, resettlement placement, and short- and long-term benefits. The USRAP coordinates the Departments of Homeland Security, State, and Health and Human Services to ensure the applicants are streamlined through the bureaucracy, and stakeholders complete necessary security and resettlement requirements. Non-profit US-based resettlement agencies manage the receptions and several benefits programs.

In coordination with the US Department of State's Bureau of Population, Refugee, and Migration (PRM), the IOM will arrange the flight and an interest-free loan to the SIV-holders. The loan must be paid by the SIV holder, in full, after 42 months, and is paid to the resettlement agency.

The assistance package for SIV-holders are similar to that provided to asylees and refugees. The R&P program covers the first 30-90 days and will address immediate needs. USRAP will provide medical and life supporting programs via HHS's Office of Refugee Resettlement (ORR) for the first eight months after arrival. In the event the applicant requires loan assistance, IOM serves as the loan provider.

The DoS's R&P program are administered by one of nine non-governmental agencies that have over 200 affiliated field and satellite offices across the US. Before departing from overseas, applicants will be assigned to one of these resettlement agencies, also known as voluntary agencies or VOLAGs. They will be given information about their final destination and the affiliate office that will handle their case. During the first 30-90 days, VOLAGS are responsible for locating and securing housing and groceries, buying and transporting necessary furniture and clothing, and assistance with medical, social, and employment services. They also assist SIV holders in applying for ORR benefits.

Appendix B

Organizational Structure of Refugee Resettlement

There are a variety of public and private agencies at the federal and state levels that collaborate to support the resettlement of asylum seekers, parolees, refugees, and SIV holders. Figure B.1 shows the three main federal agencies involved. SIV holders are by law provided with the same assistance as refugees.

Figure B.1: Main federal agencies involved in the resettlement of SIV holders

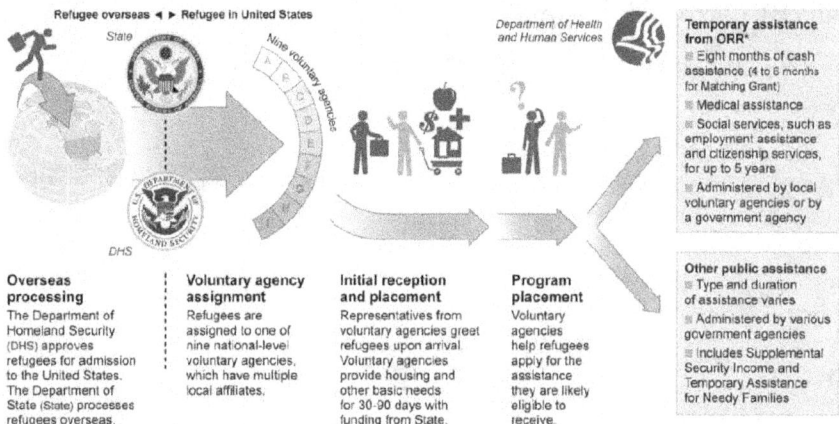

Refugee overseas ◀ ▶ Refugee in United States

State

Nine voluntary agencies

Department of Health and Human Services

DHS

Temporary assistance from ORR*
- Eight months of cash assistance (4 to 6 months for Matching Grant)
- Medical assistance
- Social services, such as employment assistance and citizenship services, for up to 5 years
- Administered by local voluntary agencies or by a government agency

Overseas processing
The Department of Homeland Security (DHS) approves refugees for admission to the United States. The Department of State (State) processes refugees overseas.

Voluntary agency assignment
Refugees are assigned to one of nine national-level voluntary agencies, which have multiple local affiliates.

Initial reception and placement
Representatives from voluntary agencies greet refugees upon arrival. Voluntary agencies provide housing and other basic needs for 30-90 days with funding from State.

Program placement
Voluntary agencies help refugees apply for the assistance they are likely eligible to receive.

Other public assistance
- Type and duration of assistance varies
- Administered by various government agencies
- Includes Supplemental Security Income and Temporary Assistance for Needy Families

*Fully or partially funded and administered by Department of Health and Human Services' Office of Refugee Resettlement (ORR)

Source: Government Accountability Office. (2012). *Refugee resettlement: Greater consultation with community stakeholders could strengthen program.* Retrieved from https://www.gao.gov/assets/600/592975.pdf

Federal Agencies

At the federal level, the U.S. Departments of Homeland Security (DHS), State (DoS), and Health and Human Services (HHS) are responsible for identifying eligible applicants, verifying authorization of immigration status, processing applicants abroad, and assisting immigrants upon arrival.[1] The DHS, in coordination with other law enforcement agencies, are responsible for vetting refugees for security purposes. As the INA's goal in refugee resettlement is to promote self-sufficiency, the Department of State, Population, Refugee and Migration (DoS/PRM) and the Department of Health and Human Services, Office of Refugee Resettlement (HHS/ORR) are responsible for administering programs to achieve that goal. PRM administers the Reception and Placement Program (R&P), ORR administers grants to states for social services, medical programs, and financial support.[2] Table B.1 shows the estimated available funding for the processing and resettlement of all refugees in FY 2016 and FY2017.

---

[1] US Department of State. (n.d.). *Special Immigrant Visas for Iraqis - Who were employed by/on behalf of the US government.* Retrieved from https://travel.state.gov/content/visas/en/immigrate/iraqis-work-for-us.html

[2] Bruno, A. (2011). *US refugee resettlement assistance.* Congressional Research Service. Retrieved from https://fas.org/sgp/crs/row/R41570.pdf

Table B.1: Estimated Funding for Refugee Processing and Resettlement FY2016 and FY2017 ($ Millions)

Agency	Estimated FY2016 Availability	Estimated FY2017 Availability
Department of Homeland Security		
United States Citizenship and Immigration Services		
Refugee Processing[1]	$50.0	$67.8
Department of State		
Bureau of Population, Refugees, and Migration		
Refugee Admissions[2, 3]	$656.6	$634.5
Department of Health and Human Services		
Office of Refugee Resettlement		
Refugee Resettlement[4]	$720.9	$841.9
Estimated Total Availabilities	$1,427.5	$1,544.2

Source: U.S. Department of State Office of Population, Refugees, and Migration.

[1]FY 2016: Includes cost factors to reflect Headquarters' facilities rent related to the refugee resettlement program, projected staffing enhancements, and following-to-join refugee processing, in addition to certain ICASS costs.

[2]FY 2016: Includes FY2016 Migration and Refugee Assistance

(MRA) appropriation of $462.7 million, $70 million in Emergency Refugee and Migration Assistance (ERMA) funding, $44.5 million in PRM carryover from FY 2015, $64.4 million in projected IOM loan collections/carryover, and an estimate of $15 million in prior year MRA recoveries. A portion of these funds will be carried forward into FY 2017.

[3]FY 2017: Includes FY2017 MRA budget request of $567.5 million, $61 million in projected IOM loan collections/carryover, and an estimate of $6 million in prior year MRA recoveries. Additional funds carried forward from FY 2016 will be available in FY 2017.

[4]FY 2016 and FY 2017: HHS's Office of Refugee Resettlement's (ORR) refugee assistance and services are also provided to asylees, Cuban and Haitian entrants, certain Amerasians from Vietnam, victims of a severe form of trafficking who have received certification or eligibility letters from ORR, certain family members who are accompanying or following to join victims of severe forms of trafficking, and some victims of torture, as well as Iraqi and Afghan Special Immigrants and their spouses and unmarried children under the age of 21. The estimated funding for these groups is included here. This category does not include costs associated with the Unaccompanied Children's Program, Temporary Assistance for Needy Families (TANF), Medicaid, Supplemental Security Income programs, or the Victims of Trafficking. These estimates do not include any prior year carryover funding.

Department of Homeland Security

The Department of Homeland Security (DHS) has two functions in the resettlement process. In the initial application process, DHS conducts a background investigation that is completed before the visa is issued. Upon arrival in the U.S., SIV holders are granted Legal Permanent Residency (LPR) status and can apply for citizenship after five years. In addition, when the SIV holder is in the U.S. and applying for citizenship, as the Customs and Immigration Service (CIS) will accept and adjudicate naturalization.

The law requires that Special Immigrants Visa applicants must be cleared through the Department of Homeland Security before being granted the SIV.[3] To initiate the process, the Department of Homeland Security, Customs and Immigration Service (CIS) processes the application for a SIV at the start of the process. Following the letter of recommendation from the Chief of Mission, DHS will initiate a background check. Once the background checks are successfully completed, DHS will notify the National Visa Center which will continue the processing of the SIV application.[4]

Special Immigrants can apply for naturalization and become US

---

[3] US Customs and Immigration Service. (n.d.). 22.3 *Special Immigrants*. Retrieved from https://www.uscis.gov/ilink/docView/AFM/HTML/AFM/0-0-0-1/0-0-0-6330/0-0-0-7696.html. This is described in detail in Appendix A.
[4] US Department of State, *Special Immigrant Visas for Iraqis*

citizens after five years. To successfully become a US citizen, the applicant must be of good moral character, have continuous residence in the US, knowledge of the US government, and basic English reading, writing and language skills. The process involves completion of an application, payment of fees, passing an English language and civic exam, and an interview with CIS. Once these have all been successfully completed, the individual then takes an oath of allegiance.[5]

Department of State

The Department of State (DoS) serves two vital roles in the SIV process. At embassies and consulates abroad, the DoS conducts the final interview and issuance of the SIV prior to entrance into the U.S. Further, DoS is charged with managing the Reception and Placement Program (R&P). Because the U.S. Department of State is at the forefront of the visa issuance, R&P initiates and coordinates domestic resettlement agencies for placement inside the continental U.S. Led by the DoS, stakeholders meet yearly to evaluate a long-term strategy based upon the previous year's resettlement, funding, and resources available. In addition, there is a weekly meeting with the DoS and leadership from the resettlements agencies to nominate SIV holders for

[5] US Citizenship and Immigration Services. (n.d.). *Citizenship through naturalization*. US Citizenship and Immigration Services. Retrieved from: https://www.uscis.gov/us-citizenship/citizenship-through-naturalization

available sponsors.

The R&P program provides short-term, immediate resettlement assistance to SIV holders upon arrival. Current SIV applicants are required to apply for resettlement prior to departing Iraq or Afghanistan. When they choose to participate in the R&P program, applicants are placed with one of nine resettlement agencies.

Under the R&P program, the resettlement agency supplies the SIV holder with 30-90 days of assistance that includes lodging for the first 30 days, basic housing necessities, and a minimal amount of cash.[6] The resettlement agency receives a grant from the DoS/PRM to provide these services. Table B.2 shows the history of funding provided by DoS/PRM to resettlement agencies.

---

[6] US Department of State. (2017). *Refugee Benefits Election Form*. Retrieved from
https://travel.state.gov/content/dam/visas/SIVs/SIV_Refugee_Benefits_Election_ Form_2017_(English).pdf

Table B.2 Funds for Resettlement Agencies*

Fiscal Year	Obligated Funds ($ Millions)
FY2006	$49.9
FY2007	$56.9
FY2008	$67.9
FY2009	$90.0
FY2010	$141.9
FY2011	$127.0
FY2012	$138.2
FY2013	$159.0
FY2014	$184.4
FY2015	$185.3
FY2016	$277.6

Source: Bureau of Population, Refugee, and Migration, US Department of State
*Includes Refugees, Asylum, Parole, and Special Immigrant Visa

SIV applicants are not required to register for assistance, however there are consequences for opting out of support. For example, an Iraqi SIV holder may have family members located in Florida. However, because the R&P program typically does not permit SIV holders to select their resettlement location, the SIV holder may forfeit R&P assistance if they reject the settlement location provided by the agency assigned to them. PRM and resettlement agencies are budget sensitive, especially at is relates to housing costs. In order to maximize efficiency, resettlement agencies attempt to identify cities with housing availability, low cost of living, employment opportunities, and other considerations when selecting settlement locations.[7]

PRM's narrow scope in the resettlement process ends 90 days after the SIV holder arrives in the U.S. The resettlement agency's funding and services from PRM are for initial placement in an apartment and transition. Prior to 2010, the grants provided by DoS to resettlement agencies for one incoming foreign national was $900. The per capita grant was increased to $1,800 in 2010. After 90 days of assistance, the grant from DoS/PRM to the resettlement agency ends.

Department of Health and Human Services

With a limited budget and dispersed organizations, the Office of Refugee Resettlement (ORR) in the Department of Health and Human Services (HHS), is responsible for funding a variety of services and assistance to states, resettlement agencies, and in some cases directly to SIV holders. With the ultimate goal self-sufficiency, the suite of services provided by ORR includes access to medical care, financial support, and social services. In most cases, ORR does not directly perform these functions but rather serves as a grantor to non-

---

[7] Office of Refugee Resettlement. (2015, September 14). *The U.S. Refugee Resettlement Program – an overview*. Retrieved from https://www.acf.hhs.gov/orr/resource/the-us-refugee-resettlement-program-an-overview; US Department of State, *Refugee Benefits Election Form*

governmental, state, or federal agencies across the U.S.[8]

The goal of refugee resettlement (including for SIV holders) is to achieve "self-sufficiency" as quickly as possible. Self-sufficiency is not explicitly defined in the INA. Minimizing dependence on public assistance is referenced several times in the INA. The ORR regulations for the Refugee Resettlement Program define it as "earning a total family income at a level that enables a family unit to support itself without receipt of a cash assistance grant."[9] Employment related services are primary focus of funding according to the HHS/ORR regulations. In addition, English language instruction, limited financial assistance, access to medical care, and social services are also provided. The INA also explicitly requires assistance be provided on an equal basis to women as well as men. It is important to note that the budget for these services covers assistance for all asylees and refugees and not just SIV holders.[10]

Financial Support. As appropriated by Congress, the monetary financial assistance programs for immigrants are the Temporary Assistance for Needy Families (TANF), Refugee Cash Assistance (RCA), and Supplemental Security Income (SSI). It is important to note, only immigrants with children qualify for TANF. SSI assistance

---

[8] Bruno, *US refugee resettlement assistance*
[9] 45 CFR §400.2
[10] Bruno, *US refugee resettlement assistance*

is available for up to seven years but is limited to the low-income, aged, and disabled. TANF assistance is available for up to five years. For those who do not qualify for TANF, RCA is available for up to eight months.

To be eligible for RCA, SIV holders must register with the state employment service, participate in the jobs program, and accept jobs offered by the employment service. The assistance amount and eligibility at the state level is determined by the state refugee coordinator. Funding for services is neither constant nor guaranteed. Depending on the federal budget and allocation of funds, some programs and services may not be sustained year-to-year.[11]

Medical assistance. Medical assistance, in the form of Medicaid, is provided to the SIV holders for seven years. For SIV holders who do not qualify for Medicaid, Refugee Medical Assistance (RMA) is an option and available for up to eight months. In states that have accepted matching federal funds under the Affordable Care Act, Medicaid will typically insure SIV holders beyond the eight-month window if needed. However, states may, and often do, cover SIV holders with state plans as an alternative.[12]

At a minimum, ORR provides the state refugee coordinator and

---

[11] Government Accountability Office, *Iraqi refugees and Special Immigrant Visa holders face challenges*
[12] Bruno, *US refugee resettlement assistance*

state health coordinator with eight months of Medicaid coverage or parallel coverage by a different insurer. Beyond that period, the SIV holder will be uninsured unless the state has additional coverage programs.[13] For example, California has accepted Medicaid expansion, as a part of the Affordable Care Act, and is able to insure SIV holders beyond the eight months if needed. Because of the decentralized approach to medical care systems and the Supreme Court decision striking down the mandatory expansion of Medicaid under the Affordable Care Act, access to medical care, insurance coverage, and services available differ from state to state.

Social Services. In order to support self-sufficiency, and particularly employment, ORR also provides funding for child daycare, recertification training, English language classes, and transportation. ORR's objective is to adjust and integrate immigrants into the local job market. The funding from ORR to the states is accomplished by a grant-based formula. Funds are allocated from ORR to the states based upon the number of refugees living in a particular state. SIV holders are eligible for social services for up to five years with the exception of food assistance, which is available indefinitely.[14] Table B.3 shows the history of funding to ORR for these programs.

---

[13] Government Accountability Office, *Iraqi refugees and Special Immigrant Visa holders face challenges*
[14] Bruno, *US refugee resettlement assistance*. As of this writing, the current limits are 7 years subject to funding availability.

Table B.3: ORR appropriations by program ($ in millions)

Programs	FY 08	FY 09	FY 10	FY 11	FY 12	FY 13	FY 14	FY 15	FY 16	FY 17
Transitional & Medical Svc	$296	$282	$353	$352	$323	$401	$391	$383	$490	$490
Social Services	$154	$154	$154	$153	$124	$149	$149	$149	$149	$155
Preventive Health	$4	$4	$4	$4	$4	$4	$4	$4	$4	$4
Targeted Assistance	$48	$48	$48	$48	$28	$47	$47	$47	$47	$47
Total Funding	**$502**	**$488**	**$559**	**$557**	**$479**	**$601**	**$591**	**$583**	**$690**	**$696**

Source: Office of Refugee Resettlement, Department of Health and Human Services

Resettlement Agencies

Resettlement Agencies, also known as Volunteer Agencies (or Volags), provide a variety of services in the resettlement process. There are nine DoS approved resettlement agencies who can apply for grants from HHS and DoS for resettlement services and assistance (see Table B.4 for the list). Resettlement agencies are the face of the U.S. for incoming immigrants. They have been doing this since the arrival of South Vietnamese in Guam. Volags remain as the vehicle for accepting and placing foreign nationals throughout the US. The resettlement services provided by the nine resettlement agencies make up a small fraction of these agencies' overall community service mission. The nine approved resettlement centers have affiliates in multiple field offices and hundreds of satellite offices throughout the US.

Table B.4: Nine Approved Resettlement Agencies

Church World Service (CWS)

Ethiopian Community Development Council (ECDC)

Episcopal Migration Ministries (EMM)

World Relief Corporation (WR)

United States Conference of Catholic Bishops (USCCB)

Lutheran Immigration and Refugee Services (LIRS)

US Committee for Refugees and Immigrants (USCRI)

International Rescue Committee (IRC)

Hebrew Immigrant Aid Society (HIAS)

NOTE: Although several of the organizations are religiously affiliated, proselytizing is strictly prohibited.

In partnership with the DoS/R&P, resettlement agencies meet weekly at the DoS's office in Washington D.C. to forecast arrivals, family dynamics, and available resources. Based upon a variety of factors, resettlement agencies accept incoming SIV holders. They are then responsible for the duties outlined in the grant provided by the DoS. In a cooperative agreement with DoS, the resettlement agency becomes the sponsor of the SIV holder.

Upon agreement of sponsorship, the resettlement agency in Washington coordinates with affiliate organizations in 190 communities throughout the US. Within the cooperative agreement, affiliate organizations are responsible for meeting the SIV applicant at the airport, securing lodging, basic clothing, food, and furnishings.

Beyond the material items provided, sponsoring agencies assist arrivals in obtaining SSI assistance, registration for school, directions on where to shop for groceries, and any other special needs.

Resettlement agencies receive grant funding from various sources to fulfill sponsorship duties. Initially, the DoS provides grants for sponsorship coordination and reception. Services beyond the initial 30-90 day resettlement period belong to ORR via agreements with state and non-governmental refugee coordinators.[15]

State Refugee Coordinator

At the state government level, governors and the legislature can fund a state refugee coordinator position that in turn oversees the grants and supplemental funds provided by the state. Typically, the state-funded refugee coordinator reports to the governor or state level health and human services agency. In states that do not fund the position, one of the nine resettlement agencies serves as the default refugee coordinator.[16]

There are 38 states where a refugee coordinator is appointed by either the legislature or governor. In this instance, the state may also

---

[15] US Department of State. (2017). *The Reception and Placement Program.* Retrieved from https://www.state.gov/j/prm/ra/receptionplacement/

[16] US Department of Health and Human Services. (n.d.). *Wilson-Fish Alternative Program Guidelines.* Retrieved from https://www.acf.hhs.gov/orr/resource/wilson-fish-alternative-program-guidelines

provide additional funds for resettlement services. The state coordinator may also acquire and provide funding to local resettlement agencies. In most cases, the state refugee coordinators serve as a conduit to a variety of immigration service agencies.

In the 12 states that have not appointed a refugee coordinator, the Wilson-Fish program is the alternative structure. In 1984, the Wilson-Fish Amendment to the INA provided an alternative means for federal grants to fund resettlement in the absence of a state coordinator. Under this program, the refugee coordinator is chosen by ORR from amongst the nine resettlement agencies. The HHS is charged with the oversight and guidelines of the Wilson-Fish program.[17]

The state refugee coordinator works directly with state resettlement agencies to determine the optimal number and location of SIV holders in a particular year. Upon a proposal by the resettlement agencies, the state coordinator can agree or disagree with the proposed resettlement count for the year. However, the state refugee coordinator does not have the authority to deny or refuse a resettlement agency's placement of a SIV holder (Health and Human Services, 2015).

Mutual Assistance Associations

In dozens of states across the U.S., Mutual Assistance Associations (MAAs) exist and serve refugees and immigrant communities at the

---

[17] Ibid

local level. These organizations are typically located in areas with a high population of immigrants such as Lowell, Massachusetts, which the census reports to have the second largest population of Cambodians in the United States. The Cambodian Mutual Assistance Association of Greater Lowell was established in 1984 independent of any government initiative. Like other MAAs, it works in cooperation with public and private resettlement agencies to assist the immigrant community with language training, job placement, and navigation of the community and culture. These organizations are typically not-for-profit and rely on donations, small service fees, and grants from ORR to serve the immigrant community. ORR partners with these organizations, as funds are available, for financing and oversight of grants.[18]

---

[18] US Department of Health and Human Services. (n.d.). *Mutual Assistance Associations*. Retrieved from https://www.acf.hhs.gov/orr/resource/mutual-assistance-associations#ma

Bibliography

Blanchard, E. (2017, Feb 02). Afghan translators hope U.S. visas will arrive before the Taliban does. *Huffington Post*. Retrieved from https://www.huffingtonpost.com/entry/afghan-translators-us-visas-taliban_us_587fbcdae4b0c147f0bca672

Brownstein, R. (2018, March 8). The health-care gap between red and blue America. *The Atlantic*. Retrieved from https://www.theatlantic.com/politics/archive/2018/03/obamacare-trump/555131/

Bruno, A. (2011). *US refugee resettlement assistance.* Congressional Research Service. Retrieved from https://fas.org/sgp/crs/row/R41570.pdf

Bruno, A. (2016). *Iraqi and Afghan Special Immigrant Visa programs.* Congressional Research Service. Retrieved from https://fas.org/sgp/crs/homesec/R43725.pdf

Bruno, G. (2008, November 05). *A tribal strategy for Afghanistan.* Retrieved from Council on Foreign Relations: https://www.cfr.org/backgrounder/tribal-strategy-afghanistan

Bureau of Labor Statistics. (2012, Feb). *The recession of 2007–2009.* Retrieved from US Department of Labor: https://www.bls.gov/spotlight/2012/recession/

Bureau of Labor Statistics. (2018, January 19). *Union Members Summary*. Retrieved from https://www.bls.gov/news.release/union2.nr0.htm

Bureau of Labor Statistics. (n.d.). *Databases, tables & calculators by subject: Unemployment.* US Department of Labor. Retrieved December 6, 2017, from https://www.bls.gov/data/#unemployment

Bureau of Labor Statistics. (n.d.). *Labor Force Statistics from the Current Population Survey*. US Department of Labor. Retrieved from: https://data.bls.gov/pdq/SurveyOutputServlet

Bureau of Population, Refugees, and Migration. (n.d.). *Admissions & arrivals*. US Department of State. Retrieved from: http://www.wrapsnet.org/admissions-and-arrivals/

Coburn, N., & Sharan, T. (2016). *Out of harm's way? Perspectives of the special immigrant visa program for Afghans*. Hollings Center for International Dialogue. Retrieved from http://www.hollingscenter.org/wp-content/uploads/2016/09/SIV-Full-Report.pdf

Cohen, R. (2008). Iraq's displaced: Where to turn? *American University International Law Review, 24*(2), 301-340. Retrieved from https://www.brookings.edu/wp-content/uploads/2016/06/10_iraq_cohen.pdf

Coll, S. (2004). *Ghost wars: The secret history of the CIA, Afghanistan, and bin Laden, from the Soviet invasion to September 10, 2001*. New York: Penguin Press.

Daniels, R. (2005). *Guarding the golden door: American immigration policy and immigrants since 1882*. New York, NY: Hill & Wang.

DeSilver, D. (2015, November 19). *U.S. public seldom has welcomed refugees into country*. Pew Research Center. Retrieved from: http://www.pewresearch.org/fact-tank/2015/11/19/u-s-public-seldom-has-welcomed-refugees-into-country/

Elliott, D. (2007, Jan 14). *A lesson in history: Resettling refugees of Vietnam*. Retrieved from National Public Radio: https://www.npr.org/templates/story/story.php?storyId=6855407

Ellison, J. (2015, March 4). As war nears an end, our Afghan translators are being left behind. *The Daily Beast*. Retrieved from http://www.thedailybeast.com/articles/2012/10/21/as-war-nears-an-end-our-afghan-translators-are-being-left-behind.html

Genizi, H. (1993). *America's fair share: The admission and resettlement of displaced persons, 1945-1952.* Detroit, MI: Wayne State University Press.

Government Accountability Office. (2010). *Iraqi refugees and Special Immigrant Visa holders face challenges resettling in the United States and obtaining US government employment.* Retrieved from http://www.gao.gov/new.items/d10274.pdf

Government Accountability Office. (2012). *Refugee resettlement: Greater consultation with community stakeholders could strengthen program.* Retrieved from https://www.gao.gov/assets/600/592975.pdf

Graham, B., & Balz, D. (1996, Sep 01). Iraqi attack raises U.S. 'concern'. *The Washington Post*. Retrieved from http://www.washingtonpost.com/wp-srv/inatl/longterm/iraq/timeline/090196.htm

Grieco, E. (2003, April 01). *Iraqi immigrants in the United States.* Retrieved from Migration Policy Institute: https://www.migrationpolicy.org/article/iraqi-immigrants-united-states-0

Gropman, A. (2014, Oct 23). *Is the President authorized to attack ISIL?* Retrieved from Military Officers Association of America: http://www.moaa.org/Content/Publications-and-Media/Features-and-Columns/Think-Tank-Nation/Is-the-President-Authorized-to-Attack-ISIL-.aspx

Guillén, M. F. (2017, Dec 12). *The global economic & financial crisis: A timeline.* Philadelphia, PA: The Lauder Institute, University of Pennsylvania. Retrieved from https://lauder.wharton.upenn.edu/wp-content/uploads/2015/06/Chronology_Economic_Financial_Crisis.pdf

Hauslohner, A., & Demirjian, K. (2016, Dec 01). Afghan visa program extended despite pushback from immigration foes. *The Washington Post*. Retrieved from https://www.washingtonpost.com/news/powerpost/wp/2016/12/02/afghan-visa-program-extended-despite-pushback-from-immigration-foes/?utm_term=.7cf09dd45cb8

Hayoun, M. (2018, March 7). The Trump administration is failing to uphold its commitments to Vietnamese refugees. *Pacific Standard*. Retrieved from https://psmag.com/social-justice/the-trump-administration-is-failing-to-uphold-its-commitments-to-vietnamese-refugees

Hein, J. (1995). *From Vietnam, Laos, and Cambodia: A refugee experience in the United States*. New York: Twayne.

HSH Associates. (n.d.). *HSH's national monthly mortgage statistics: 1986 to 2016*. Retrieved December 6, 2017, from https://www.hsh.com/monthly-mortgage-rates.html

International Refugee Assistance Project. (n.d.). *Home*. Retrieved from Urban Justice Center: https://refugeerights.org/

International Rescue Committee. (2009). *Iraqi refugees in the United States: In dire straits*. New York, NY.

Iraqi Mutual Aid Society. (n.d.). *Home*. Retrieved from http://www.iraqimutualaid.org/

Johannes, C. (2017, October 6). US Kurds face detention, deportation as Trump cracks down on immigration. *Rudaw*. Retrieved from http://www.rudaw.net/english/kurdistan/10062017

Johnson, K. W. (2013). *To be a friend is fatal: The fight to save the Iraqis America left behind*. New York: Scribner.

Jones, J. (2017). Operation Provide Comfort: A forgotten mission with possible lessons for Syria. *Foreign Policy*. Retrieved from http://foreignpolicy.com/2017/02/06/operation-provide-comfort-a-forgotten-mission-with-possible-lessons-for-syria/

Karimi., H. (2010, Feburary 19). The Kurdish immigrant experience and a growing American community. *Kurdish Herald*. Retrieved from: http://ekurd.net/mismas/articles/misc2010/2/kurdsworldwide436.htm

Katz, B., & Wagner, J. (2008, June 1). *Transformative investments: Remaking American cities for a new century*. Brookings Institution. Retrieved from: https://www.brookings.edu/articles/transformative-investments-remaking-american-cities-for-a-new-century/

Kerry, J. (2014, June 2). From John Kerry: We need more visas, now, for our Afghan allies. *Los Angeles Times*. Retrieved from http://www.latimes.com/opinion/op-ed/la-oe-0602-kerry-afghan-withdrawal-20140603-story.html

Khadduri, M., & Ghareeb, E. (2001). *War in the Gulf, 1990-91: The Iraq-Kuwait conflict and its implications*. Oxford: Oxford University Press.

Kissinger, H. (2003). *Ending the Vietnam War: A history of America's involvement in and extrication from the Vietnam War*. New York: Simon & Schuster.

Levin, S. (2018, March 3). Detained and divided: how the US turned on Vietnamese refugees. *The Guardian*. Retrieved from https://www.theguardian.com/us-news/2018/mar/03/vietnamese-refugees-immigration-us-detention

Levitt, L. (2018, January 5). The Trump administration's hidden attacks on the Affordable Care Act. *The Washington Post*.

Retrieved from https://www.washingtonpost.com/opinions/the-trump-administrations-hidden-attacks-on-the-affordable-care-act/2018/01/05/bd7002da-f237-11e7-97bf-bba379b809ab_story.html?utm_term=.741f2f7c3d07

Lipson, J. G., & Meleis, A. I. (1983). Issues in health care of Middle Eastern patients. *Western Journal of Medicine, 139*(6), 854-861.

Lonsdorf, K., & Martin, P. (2016, July 06). Thousands of Afghan interpreters wait for visas as Congress squabbles. *U.S. News & World Report*. Retrieved from https://www.usnews.com/news/articles/2016-07-07/thousands-of-afghan-interpreters-wait-for-visas-as-congress-squabbles

MacroTrends. (n.d.). *Dow Jones - 100 Year Historical Chart*. Retrieved December 6, 2017, from http://www.macrotrends.net/1319/dow-jones-100-year-historical-chart

Marsh, R. E. (1980). Socioeconomic status of Indochinese refugees in the United States: Progress and problems. *Social Security Bulletin, 43*(10), 11-20.

Martin, P. (2014, May 19). *Trends in migration to the U.S.* Population Reference Bureau. Retrieved from: http://www.prb.org/Publications/Articles/2014/us-migration-trends.aspx

McCain, Shaheen, Reed & Tillis introduce bipartisan bill to authorize 2,500 additional visas for Afghan interpreters. (2017, March 02). Retrieved from Senator John McCain: https://www.mccain.senate.gov/public/index.cfm/2017/3/mccain-shaheen-reed-tillis-introduce-bipartisan-bill-to-authorize-2-500-additional-visas-for-afghan-interpreters

Moulton, S. (2016, Aug 02). *Moulton and bipartisan group of lawmakers to NDAA conferees: Support the Afghan Special*

Immigrant Visa program. Congressman Seth Moulton. Retrieved from: https://moulton.house.gov/legislative-center/moulton-and-bipartisan-group-of-lawmakers-to-ndaa-conferees-support-the-afghan-special-immigrant-visa-program/

National Commission on Terrorist Attacks upon the United States. (2004). *The 9/11 Commission report.* Washington, DC. Retrieved from http://govinfo.library.unt.edu/911/report/index.htm

National Security Council. (n.d.). *National Security Council.* Retrieved January 15, 2015, from http://www.whitehouse.gov/administration/eop/nsc/

Nixon, J. (2016). *Debriefing the president: The interrogation of Saddam Hussein.* New York, NY: Blue Rider Press.

No One Left Behind. (n.d.). *Home.* Retrieved from http://noonleft.org/

Office of Refugee Resettlement. (2015, September 14). *The U.S. Refugee Resettlement Program – an overview.* Retrieved from https://www.acf.hhs.gov/orr/resource/the-us-refugee-resettlement-program-an-overview

Packer, G. (2015, March 04). An Afghan interpreter's flight to America. *The New Yorker.* Retrieved from http://www.newyorker.com/news/daily-comment/an-afghan-interpreters-flight-to-america

Paradise, K. G. (1977). *From Vietnam to America: A chronicle of the Vietnamese immigration to the United States.* Boulder, CO: Westview Press.

Pearson, J. (2018, April 12). US seeks to deport thousands of Vietnamese protected by treaty: former ambassador. *Reuters.* Retrieved from https://www.reuters.com/article/us-usa-vietnam-deportees/u-s-seeks-to-deport-thousands-of-

vietnamese-protected-by-treaty-former-ambassador-
idUSKBN1HJ0OU

Reimers, D. M. (1983). An unintended reform: The 1965 Immigration
Act and third world immigration to the United States. *Journal
of American Ethnic History, 3*(1), 9-28.

Religious Diversity in Minnesota Initiative. (n.d.). *The Development of
Vietnamese Communities in the US*. Retrieved November 22,
2017, from http://religionsmn.carleton.edu/exhibits/show/phat-
an-temple/the-development-of-vietnamese-

Rosenfeld, J., Denice, P., & Laird, J. (2013, Aug 30). *Union decline
lowers wages of nonunion workers*. Economic Policy Institute.
Retrieved from: http://www.epi.org/publication/union-decline-
lowers-wages-of-nonunion-workers-the-overlooked-reason-
why-wages-are-stuck-and-inequality-is-growing/

Rutledge, P. (1992). *The Vietnamese experience in America.*
Bloomington, Ind.: Indiana University Press.

Safer, M. (1990). *Flashbacks on returning to Vietnam.* New York, NY:
Random House.

Sahara, A. (2009). *Operations new life/arrivals: U.S. national project
to forget the Vietnam War.* Unpublished Masters Thesis,
University of California at San Diego. Retrieved from
https://escholarship.org/uc/item/8782s7bc

Sanchez, T. (2018, April 6). Former ambassador to Vietnam: Trump
wanted me to send back refugees. *The Mercury News.*
Retrieved from
https://www.mercurynews.com/2018/04/06/former-
ambassador-to-vietnam-trump-wanted-me-to-send-back-
refugees/

Sawyer, A. M. (2017, June 22). Who are the Kurds, and why are they
in Nashville? *The Tennessean.* Retrieved from:

http://www.tennessean.com/story/news/local/2017/06/23/who-kurds-and-why-they-nashville/97706968/

Scanlan, J., & Loescher, G. (1985). *Calculated Kindness.* New York, NY: The Free Press.

Schaefer, R. T., & Schaefer, S. L. (1975). Reluctant welcome: U.S. responses to the South Vietnamese refugees. *Journal of Ethnic and Migration Studies, 4*(3), 366-370.

Schmidt, S. (2018, March 1). Vietnamese immigrants are stuck in limbo, detained indefinitely, lawsuit says. *The Washington Post.* Retrieved from https://www.washingtonpost.com/news/morning-mix/wp/2018/03/01/vietnamese-immigrants-are-stuck-in-limbo-detained-indefinitely-lawsuit-says

Sheppard, S. (2016, October 25). What the Syrian Kurds have wrought. *The Atlantic.* Retrieved from https://www.theatlantic.com/international/archive/2016/10/kurds-rojava-syria-isis-iraq-assad/505037/

Sieff, K. (2015, March 09). In Afghanistan, interpreters who helped U.S. in war denied visas; U.S. says they face no threat. *The Washington Post.* Retrieved from http://www.washingtonpost.com/world/in-afghanistan-interpreters-who-helped-us-in-war-denied-visas

Sisk, C. (2017, June 9). At least 6 former Kurdish refugees face deportation amid what activists describe as a sweep. *Nashville Public Radio.* Retrieved from http://nashvillepublicradio.org/post/least-6-former-kurdish-refugees-face-deportation-amid-what-activists-describe-sweep#stream/0

Sissons, M., & Al-Saiedi, A. (2013). *A bitter legacy: Lessons of de-Baathification in Iraq.* Washington D.C.: International Center for Transitional Justice. Retrieved from

https://www.ictj.org/sites/default/files/ICTJ-Report-Iraq-De-
Baathification-2013-ENG.pdf

Snepp, F. (2002). *Decent interval: An insider's account of Saigon's
indecent end* . New York: Random House.

The Data Center. (n.d.). *White Flight.* Retrieved from
http://www.datacenterresearch.org/pre-
katrina/tertiary/white.html

The Economist. (2017, August 31). *The roots of Afghanistan's tribal
tensions.* Retrieved from
https://www.economist.com/blogs/economist-
explains/2017/08/economist-explains-21

The List Project. (n.d.). *Iraq - 1996.* Retrieved from
http://thelistproject.org/history/iraq-1996/

The List Project to Resettle Iraqi Allies. (n.d.). *Home.* Retrieved from
http://thelistproject.org

Toosi, N. (2018, March 8). Refugee skeptic lands top State Department
refugee job. *Politico.* Retrieved from
https://www.politico.com/story/2018/03/08/andrew-veprek-
state-department-refugee-admissions-448210

United Nations High Commissioner for Refugees. (2012, August 02).
UNHCR global resettlement statistical report. Retrieved from
http://www.unhcr.org/52693bd09.html.

University of Michigan. (n.d.). *Consumer Sentiment.* St. Louis Federal
Reserve Bank. Retrieved from:
https://fred.stlouisfed.org/series/UMCSENT

US Census Bureau. (n.d.). *American Fact Finder.* Retrieved from
https://factfinder.census.gov/faces/tableservices/jsf/pages/produ
ctview.xhtml?src=bkmk

US Citizenship and Immigration Services. (n.d.). *Citizenship through naturalization*. US Citizenship and Immigration Services. Retrieved from: https://www.uscis.gov/us-citizenship/citizenship-through-naturalization

US Citizenship and Immigration Services. (n.d.). *What is humanitarian parole and how does it apply to asylum seekers?* Retrieved from https://my.uscis.gov/helpcenter/article/what-is-humanitarian-parole-and-how-does-it-apply-to-asylum-seekers

US Customs and Immigration Service. (2015, April 24). *Iraqi refugee processing fact sheet*. Retrieved from http://www.uscis.gov/humanitarian/refugees-asylum/refugees/iraqi-refugee-processing-fact-sheet

US Customs and Immigration Service. (n.d.). *22.3 Special Immigrants*. Retrieved from https://www.uscis.gov/ilink/docView/AFM/HTML/AFM/0-0-0-1/0-0-0-6330/0-0-0-7696.html

US Customs and Immigration Service. (n.d.). *Immigration and Nationality Act*. Retrieved from https://www.uscis.gov/ilink/docView/SLB/HTML/SLB/act.html

US Department of Defense. (1977). *Operation New Life/New Arrivals: US Army support to the Indochinese refugee program*.

US Department of Defense. (1997, April 15). *Operation Pacific Haven wraps up humanitarian efforts, Release No: 177-97*. Retrieved from http://archive.defense.gov/Releases/Release.aspx?ReleaseID=1218

US Department of Defense. (n.d.). *DoD Authorizes Global War on Terrorism Medals for Operation Freedom's Sentinel*. Retrieved from http://prhome.defense.gov/RFM/MPP/OEPM/Functions

US Department of Health and Human Services. (n.d.). *Mutual Assistance Associations*. Retrieved from https://www.acf.hhs.gov/orr/resource/mutual-assistance-associations#ma

US Department of Health and Human Services. (n.d.). *Wilson-Fish Alternative Program Guidelines*. Retrieved from https://www.acf.hhs.gov/orr/resource/wilson-fish-alternative-program-guidelines

US Department of Labor. (n.d.). *Women in the Labor Force*. Retrieved November 19, 2017, from https://www.dol.gov/wb/stats/NEWSTATS/facts/women_lf.htm#two

US Department of State & US Department of Homeland Security. (2018, April 2018). *Joint Department of State/Department of Homeland Security report: Status of the Iraqi special immigrant visa program.* US Department of State. Retrieved from https://travel.state.gov/content/dam/visas/SIVs/Report_of_the_Iraqi_SIV_Program-October_2017.pdf

US Department of State. (2013, May). *U.S. Refugee Admissions Program (USRAP) Frequently Asked Questions - Iraqi processing*. Retrieved from Bureau of Population, Refugees, and Migration: https://2009-2017.state.gov/j/prm/releases/factsheets/2013/210134.htm

US Department of State. (2014, May 23). *Iraqi Refugee Resettlement*. Retrieved from Bureau of Population, Refugees, and Migration: https://2009-2017.state.gov/j/prm/releases/factsheets/2014/228685.htm

US Department of State. (2016, September 15). *Proposed Refugee Admissions for Fiscal Year 2017*. Retrieved from https://www.state.gov/j/prm/releases/docsforcongress/261956.htm

US Department of State. (2017). *Refugee Benefits Election Form.* Retrieved from https://travel.state.gov/content/dam/visas/SIVs/SIV_Refugee_B enefits_Election_Form_2017_(English).pdf

US Department of State. (2017). *The Reception and Placement Program.* Retrieved from https://www.state.gov/j/prm/ra/receptionplacement/

US Department of State. (2017, Oct). *U.S. Visas.* Retrieved from: https://travel.state.gov/content/visas/en/immigrate/afghans-work-for-us.html

US Department of State. (n.d.). *Mission.* Retrieved from Bureau of Consular Affairs: https://travel.state.gov/content/travel/en/about-us.html

US Department of State. (n.d.). *Special Immigrant Visas for Iraqis - Who were employed by/on behalf of the US government.* Retrieved from https://travel.state.gov/content/visas/en/immigrate/iraqis-work-for-us.html

US Department of State. (n.d.). *The Immigration and Nationality Act of 1952 (The McCarran-Walter Act).* Retrieved from Office of the Historian: https://history.state.gov/milestones/1945-1952/immigration-act

Weed, M. C. (2015, Apr 14). *2001 Authorization for use of military force: Issues concerning its continued application.* Congressional Research Service. Retrieved from https://fas.org/sgp/crs/natsec/R43983.pdf

Wieder, R. (1995). Vietnamese American. In S. Gall, & I. Natividad (Eds.), *The Asian American almanac: A reference work on Asians in the US* (pp. 165-174). Detroit, MI: Gale Research Inc.

Woodward, B. (2004). *Plan of attack.* New York: Simon & Schuster.

Zhou, M., & Bankston, C. L. (1995). Entrepreneurship. In S. Gall, & I. Natividad (Eds.), *The Asian American almanac: A reference work on Asians in the US* (pp. 511-528). Detriot, MI: Gale Research Inc.

Zucchino, D. (2017, Feb 02). Visa ban amended to allow Iraqi interpreters into U.S. *New York Times.* Retrieved from https://www.nytimes.com/2017/02/02/world/middleeast/trump-visa-ban-iraq-interpreters.html

www.ingramcontent.com/pod-product-compliance
Lightning Source LLC
Chambersburg PA
CBHW062212270326
41930CB00009B/1720